CONTENTS

7 **Foreword**

8 **Acknowledgment**

9 **List of Lenders**

10 **Chronology**

12 **Family Album**

14 **Peter Blake**
Michael Compton

31 **Peter Blake and the Ruralists**
Nicholas Usherwood

35 **Peter Blake and the Durable Expendables**
Robert Melville

40 **List of Plates**

73 **Catalogue**

127 **Bibliography**

Cover
'Titania', 1972–4 (detail)

Frontispiece
Peter Blake 1982. Photograph taken by Terence Donovan.

PETER BLAKE

TATE GALLERY

This exhibition is dedicated to Chrissy Wilson,
my daughters Liberty and Daisy, and my family and
friends, particularly my special friend, Mani,
and everybody who is less, but better, than perfect.

*   *   *

Lenders and others have been thanked elsewhere in the
catalogue but here I would particularly like to thank
Michael Compton and Caroline Odgers for their support
and all the work they have done on the exhibition.

ISBN 0 905005 14 7
Published by order of the Trustees
for the exhibition of 9 February–20 March 1983
Copyright © The Tate Gallery 1983
Second impression 1983

Published by the Tate Gallery Publications Department,
Millbank, London SW1P 4RG
Designed by Sue Fowler
Printed by Balding + Mansell Limited, Wisbech, Cambs

Photographic Credits
Prudence Cuming Associates
Tate Gallery Photographic Department
John Webb

Organised with support from **CAPITAL** RADIO·194

PETER
BLAKE

FOREWORD

Peter Blake is the most British of artists; his feelings, subjects and types are all archetypally British. Yet at the same time his art is thoroughly individual. His painting has no parallel in Britain just as it has no equivalent abroad. It combines a brilliant technique with a personal approach which is strong, attractive and all his own.

This is Peter Blake's first London retrospective and will include early work done at art school, images painted in the sixties when he was acclaimed as one of the founders of British Pop Art and the group of works painted in the seventies when he was living in the country. He has been working on a number of new works especially for the exhibition.

The exhibition has been selected by Michael Compton, the Tate Gallery's Keeper of Museum Services, who has also written the catalogue. We are very grateful to Nicholas Usherwood for his contribution and to Robert Melville for allowing us to reprint his article from *Motif*.

The owners of works have been extremely generous and co-operative. We should like to express our warmest thanks to Her Majesty Queen Elizabeth II, and to all the lenders, including those who have wished to remain anonymous.

Our greatest thanks are to Peter Blake himself who has given a great deal of time and attention to every aspect of the exhibition. We would like to thank Chrissy Wilson for her help and in particular for her work on the Sculpture Park.

We are most grateful to Capital Radio for their support. Leslie Waddington has generously contributed towards the cost of colour plates in the catalogue. For help in organising the exhibition we are particularly grateful to the following – Francis Greenacre of the Bristol City Art Gallery, Robert Fraser, Eric Lister of the Portal Gallery and the staff of Waddington Galleries, in particular Louisa Riley-Smith and Andrea Hill.

When the exhibition closes at the Tate, a reduced version will be shown at the Kestner Gesellschaft, Hanover, from 22 April until 12 June, with support from the British Council.

Alan Bowness
Director

ACKNOWLEDGMENT

The music played in this exhibition has been brought to the Tate by Capital Radio, and we are delighted to be associated with Peter Blake's work in this way.

The idea of Capital providing music designed to be in sympathy with the pictures seems particularly appropriate. Pop art and pop music often share similar inspirations and in their different ways both Capital and Peter Blake have been 'pop' innovators. To millions of Londoners 'Capital Radio 194' means the best in popular music, and this retrospective exhibition of Peter Blake's work is a tribute to his outstanding reputation.

Capital has always striven for inventive ways for radio to serve audiences and artists, and our coverage of classical as well as popular music, reviews of books and the arts enjoys wide recognition. In that same spirit, we welcome the opportunity to bring the musical 'fourth' dimension to the galleries and we wish the exhibition every success.

Nigel Walmsley
Managing Director, Capital Radio

LIST OF LENDERS

Her Majesty The Queen 174

Klaus and Gertrude Anschel 208
Ann Arnold 98b
Graham Arnold 98c
Arts Council of Great Britain 20, 52

Richard Brown Baker 96
Baltimore Museum of Art 202
Agnes and Frits Becht 79, 201
Bedford, Cecil Higgins Art Gallery 222
Erik and Lilott Berganus 12, 110, 210
San Lorenzo Restaurant 149
Daisy Blake 122
Peter Blake 22, 72, 86, 89, 98a, 99, 100,
    101, 103, 104, 105, 106, 107, 108,
    112, 114, 124, 126, 127, 128, 129,
    130, 133, 134, 137, 138, 177, 179,
    181, 182, 183, 211, 220
Terry Blake 45
Mr & Mrs Terry Blake 224
Mark Boxer 78
Bristol Museum and Art Gallery 97
Mrs Neville Burston 170, 227

Carlisle Museum and Art Gallery 4
Patrick Caulfield 209
Mr Chow 60
Brian Clarke 188
Cologne, Museum Ludwig 50
Fleur Cowles 17, 21

Robyn Denny 141
Deweer Art Gallery 153, 159
Jim Dine 115

Annelotte Elbrecht 145
Judith Elliott 113

Galerie Forni 93
Frankfurt, Galerie Meyer-Ellinger 65,
    81, 178, 229a
Robert Fraser Gallery 185, 186, 187,
    189, 191, 194, 196, 197, 198, 199

Gilbert and George 117
Fundação Calouste Gulbenkian,
    Lisbon 36

Harveys of Bristol 231
Miriam Haworth 144
Adrian Heath 70
David Hockney 102, 116
Howard Hodgkin 104a
Gordon and Jo House 3, 121, 143, 229
City of Kingston upon Hull
    Museums 49

Jaguar Cars Ltd 233
Paul E. Johnen 180

Ian Kennedy Martin 109
R.B. Kitaj 120

Leeds City Art Galleries 41

Paul and Linda McCartney 82
Mr and Mrs Robert Melville 27, 125
Bryan Morrison 32

Shirley Norfolk 2

Annie Ovenden 98e

A & F Pears Ltd 228
Tom Phillips 123

Private collection 8, 11, 16, 22, 23, 25,
    26, 28, 31, 40, 42, 43, 46, 48, 51, 53,
    54, 56, 58, 59, 61, 62, 63, 66, 71, 84,
    88, 91, 95, 118, 119, 131, 132, 136,
    139, 140, 146, 147, 148, 150, 151,
    154, 155, 156, 157, 158, 160, 161,
    162, 163, 169, 172, 173, 176, 192,
    195, 203, 204, 205, 217, 218, 223, 226

Everard Read Collection 90
Rotterdam, Museum Boymans – Van
    Beuningen 73, 171
Royal College of Art 9, 10, 80

Sheffield City Art Galleries 6
Robert Shuman 225
Richard Smith 24
Giorgio Soavi 207
Erich Sommer 57, 184
Hans Sonnenberg 75
Mrs Jinty Stephenson 7
Mrs Stoutzker 5, 14, 67

Tate Gallery 15, 19, 29, 33, 34, 37, 55
Thyssen-Bornemisza Collection 77

Victoria and Albert Museum 35, 142
Vienna, Museum moderner Kunst 44

Anya and Laura Waddington 164-8
Waddington Galleries 1, 13, 38, 39, 64,
    68, 69, 74, 76, 83, 85, 87, 92, 94, 98d,
    111, 135, 152, 175, 190, 193, 200,
    206, 212–16, 219, 221, 230, 232, 234
Waddington and Piccadilly
    Galleries 98f
Whitworth Art Gallery 47
Wolverhampton Art Gallery 18
Mrs Garth Wood 30

CHRONOLOGY

1932
Born 25 June, in Dartford, Kent

1946–9
Gravesend Technical College and School of Art
Junior Art Department

1949–51
Gravesend School of Art

1950
Accepted by the Royal College of Art

1951–3
National Service in R.A.F.

1953–6
Royal College of Art – First Class Diploma 1956

1956–7
Travelled in Holland, Belgium, France, Italy and
Spain on a Leverhulme Research Award to study
popular art

1960–62
Taught at St Martin's School of Art

1960–63
Taught at Harrow School of Art

1961–4
Taught at Walthamstow School of Art

1961

Featured in Ken Russell's B.B.C. 'Monitor' film 'Pop goes the easel'.

Won Junior prize at John Moore's Liverpool exhibition

1962

One-man exhibition, Portal Gallery, London

1963

Married Jann Haworth

Visited Los Angeles to do a portfolio of drawings for *The Sunday Times*

1964–76

Taught at Royal College of Art

1965

One-man exhibition, Robert Fraser Gallery, London

1968

Daughter, Juliette Liberty Blake, born

1969

One-man exhibition, Robert Fraser Gallery, London; retrospective exhibition, City Art Gallery, Bristol; moved to Wellow, Avon (until 1979)

1973–4

Retrospective exhibition in Amsterdam, Hamburg, Brussels and Arnhem

1974

Daughter, Daisy Blake, born; appointed A.R.A. (Associate member of the Royal Academy)

1975

Founder-member of the Brotherhood of Ruralists, with Jann Haworth, Ann and Graham Arnold, David Inshaw, and Annie and Graham Ovenden; first exhibited as a group in the Royal Academy Summer exhibition, 1976; major group exhibition at Arnolfini Gallery, Bristol, 1981, travelling to Birmingham, Glasgow and London (Camden Arts Centre)

1977

One-man exhibition, 'Souvenirs and Samples', Waddington and Tooth Galleries I, London

1979

Separated from Jann Haworth and returned to London (divorced 1981). Has lived with Chrissy Wilson since 1980

1981

Appointed R.A. (full member of the Royal Academy)

1983

Retrospective exhibition, Tate Gallery, London, travelling to Kestner-Gesellschaft, Hanover

Peter's mother, Betty, 1928

Peter's father, Kenneth (left), 1931

Peter, 5 months old

Peter, Margate, 1933

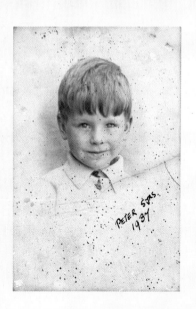

Peter, 5 years old, 1937

Peter and sister Shirley,
evacuated 1942

R.A.F. (centre back), 1951

Liberty, 1981

Peter and Joe Tilson, Spain, 1957

Daisy, 1980

The Brotherhood of Ruralists, 1976

Chrissy Wilson and Peter, 1981

PETER BLAKE

Blake is an artist whose work seems to spring in the most direct way from his interests and affections. It shows great skill of hand and a unique and fertile imagination. It is genuinely popular but appeals also to some of the most acute connoisseurs, collectors and curators of our day.

It is possible to distinguish periods and groups of works within the luxuriant whole, although there are many overlappings and cross connections, and some items do not fit in. The first group comprises graphics, executed at Gravesend Technical College and School of Art as a teenage student between 1946 and 1951. Although these are juvenile works and there are almost no examples in the exhibition one may find in them the germs both of the technical accomplishment of the mature painter and of some of his themes and devices.

The next two groups were executed at the Royal College and in short periods before and after. They comprise an 'autobiographical' series of boys and girls in their natural environment and an exotic series of circus or fairground figures.

The autobiographical series, which establishes the realist or naturalistic thread in his development, culminates in the 'Self Portrait with Badges' 1961. It is not carried on until, quite transformed, it appears in the watercolours of his children and the self portrait with David Hockney and Howard Hodgkin of 1981–3 (Cat. nos. 104-106).

The circus figures similarly establish the thread of fantasy. They are transformed into the wrest-lers and strippers which continue intermittently from 1961 to today. The typical form of these, however, crystallised in about 1963 and has not greatly altered.

The next group comprises the Pop works which fall between the naturalistic and fantasy works. Some are devoted to real film or music personalities and are painted in a way that reflects their sources in Pop ephemera. Others are collaged out of the same material. Some deal with more general themes like love, or being a fan. Still others focus directly on the products and styles of commercial folk art, decorations, toys, cigarette cards etc. which are assembled in the work. A last, episodic sub-group refers back to high Pop art itself. Blake has always been interested in both coincidental resemblances and conscious mutual borrowings between fine and commercial art. These fall mainly between 1959 and 1963.

A related series of works are called 'Postcards'. These derive quite directly from Blake's Lever-hulme Research Award to study popular ephemera. They represent a European, even a Latin notion of love rather than an American, and comprise collages of cards and paintings based directly on such cards. They are mostly from the period 1959–65 although there is a series of prints of 1969.

In the same periods there are some studies of fruit, flowers and pebbles but the iconography is essentially urban, British and quite distinct from the 'highbrow' imagery of other artists.

In 1969 Blake moved to the country with his wife and daughter, Liberty, and later formed with other artists 'The Brotherhood of Ruralists' which is discussed in a separate essay. His iconography became rural and he was preoccupied with themes of childhood and fairy-tale both of which had occupied him earlier but much less exclusively. This group comprises both real works: portraits and landscapes, and imaginary: fiction and fairies.

Meanwhile his technical accomplishment had evolved to the point where he was able to give the most compelling reality to his imagination. There was an element of fully acknowledged nostalgia in his art but the value he placed on his skill caused him to be invited to become first an ARA and then an RA which he accepted. On the other hand the uniqueness of his imagination, some shared sensibilities and friendships determined that he continued to be regarded internationally as a leading figure of modern art. Such a position is almost unique in his generation, although a relatively recent blurring of the lines of demarcation defending modernism have made it seem less improbable.

After separation from his wife, he returned to urban life in 1979, revisiting Los Angeles, which he had celebrated in 1963, before David Hockney, and settling in London. He has carried on individual works and series begun in his ruralist phase, he has completed certain works begun before then and has begun others, especially the group of three on the theme of Los Angeles.

It has become more than ever clear that there is only a difference in category and form between the urban and the rural figures, the imagination that produces them and the hand that conjures them into existence are just the same.

One group that I have passed over is that of the souvenirs in which he has paid his respects to artists and other friends that he admires. These are even more personal and direct than the works which celebrate real or fictional characters. The group springs from his habit of exchanging work with fellow artists and of giving drawings or other small items to people who have bought paintings (plastic toys in the cornflakes packet). It may be considered to have begun with the work that also began the series of Pop and Musical Works in this exhibition – a painting of the black, glamorous and all round entertainer, Sammy Davis Jr. that Blake painted in 1960 and took to the star's hotel. There it was handed to the porter, for Blake did not aspire to be able to present it personally. It has since then quite disappeared.

Finally there are the works in progress that point to the continuity of his ideas and way of working. Among them at the time of writing is the 'Sculpture Park' in which he directs his attention to contemporary art, its styles and characteristics.

* * *

One of the most obvious features of this story is that Blake shares with people both in and outside the art world an interest in toys, films, illustrated books, magazines, movies, pop music, advertisements and all the other products of commerce and the media, old and new, especially those that comprise images of one sort or another. They regularly form part of the material of his work. He is of the generation of the Pop artists and, because his work did indeed show links with the popular arts, he was in effect coopted into the group as it was publicly represented. He certainly learnt something from that but finally he cannot be thought of as a Pop artist. His work has remained too personal, it has roots in other traditions, especially those of historic fine art, graphic art and illustration; 'pop' imagery has only been a part of it.

The difference between Blake and such a definitive Pop artist as Lichtenstein is illustrated in the fact that, when Blake does more or less deliberately imitate the manner of an existing flat image, that is in his 'Postcards', he chooses images which are very old-fashioned and quite without violence or cartoon quality. On the other hand when he turns to American stars of music and screen he places them in a framework of door and locker panels or other devices that are obviously part of the context of British things and places.

His style is naturalistic in essence, even when he is painting fictions or fantasies. Likewise his use of popular imagery is natural, not a device to be used in the art game. It does not conform to the theories that have been put forward to validate Pop art. He does not systematically simulate the styles of the mass media or use them as a means of smuggling three-dimensional images into a painting by representing a two-dimensional object such as a frame of a comic. His work is not orientated to America but to Britain. He is of course very well aware of the whole range of contemporary art and is prepared to defend his position within it. His works contain occasional witty references to contemporary modernism, some of his subjects are notably contemporary but he carries on unashamedly the traditions of the past, and seems to stand aside from the currents of art fashion. He can produce images which are powerful today and will be powerful tomorrow precisely because they reflect so exactly the character of an artist who, like all of us, has private and public attitudes, a past, a heritage and a present.

He is neither wholly a naturalistic, nor a fantastic nor an abstract artist. That is, when he makes a painting, he does not simply choose a view, a model or a subject and paint what he sees, neither does he form an image in his mind and simply paint that. Of course he does not paint purely formal or emotive masses of colour, although his pictures are carefully composed, and his repertoire of brush stroke types is immensely varied and expressive.

*   *   *

Blake's way of working is in some ways close to that of a film maker or novelist and has much in common with the methods of the history and imaginative painters of the Renaissance and the nineteenth century, whose function has in a sense been taken over by film makers. His paintings may be conceived and elaborated in his mind for many years before he begins to paint them and may take many more years to complete. In fact most are plainly never quite complete. He would prefer to paint one great complex work in perfect detail but, in the meantime, is content to bring certain parts of major pictures to a level of the most complete realisation that he can achieve in his medium and to paint in detail very small works which may be considered parts of a complex series or of a whole.

The original idea for a painting may be the sight of an image, an object or another work of art. It may be a book or something in a newspaper or magazine that catches his attention. It may be an event or the need to find a form for his feelings about some aspect of his life. It may be any combination of these. During a period of gestation, that will certainly overlap with periods of thinking about or working on other paintings, he will begin to collect material for the picture. If the painting springs from an image – say a picture from a magazine, a postcard or an old photograph – this will be joined by other images. Some may be photographs of figures posed and taken specially, but generally they are collected. Blake forms collections of things that he likes for their own sake; following the graphic artists' training that he had at Gravesend, he also collects and classifies images as material to be used in potential works; he collects items that he can associate with the theme of a particular work, which may be two-dimensional representations, like plates from a magazine, or three-dimensional, like toys or souvenirs. They may be badges, lettering, frames, decorative borders, fragments of costume or anything that has style or character. Occasionally a part will be specially made by a friend.

All these have to be consistent with the basic theme, so that, if this is a person, the object must plausibly belong to that person or illustrate a part of that person's biography. Such a person takes on in Blake's mind sufficient detail and history to account for everything in the picture, becoming a complex fiction, a character. Even if the subject is a real person, he or she will be treated as a myth, a figment of the media. The character will probably have a name and the story may be elaborated before much has been actually painted. If the picture remains for very long in his studio, the character may be affected by the development of other pictures, and sometimes by changes in Blake's life or attitudes, but it remains essentially the same 'person'. In so far as it has this consistency it has an independence. Many playwrights have spoken of having characters in their heads, in the same way, waiting for a play to be written about them.

Naturally development will take place fastest when Blake is actually working on the painting, but the idea has sufficient strength to retain its identity for years during which little or no actual painting takes place so that he can go back to a picture set aside long ago and take it up immediately. In this he is helped by his method, by the collection of images which form the material for the work and by the format-type which will be fairly consistent for a series.

The material for the painting will be mainly photographic: actual photographs or printed images. He very rarely copies these directly and completely and does not square them up. He does sometimes use an epidiascope to project the image on to the canvas or panel and he may use tracing for the same purpose. In any case the image has to be fully realised – just as if he were looking at it in the flesh. It is very difficult to distinguish what has been invented or painted from life from that which comes from photographic or other pre-existing images. The process of completion will typically begin with the most interesting and expressive features, generally the eyes (or one eye), nose and mouth. As they are corrected or redefined they tend to grow. The body and limbs grow likewise from inside to out, both in two and in three dimensions so that the figure seems literally to put on flesh or to be conjured into being by magic. After the head, the trunk is realised, then the shoulders, hips, arms and legs, finally the hands and feet. If certain essential elements are sufficiently realised the rest may be left in varying states of completion. Blake is quite happy to exhibit and sell works in this condition, although each is in principle capable of completion down to the last detail. The fine detail of crucial parts implies the completion of the rest.

The length of time it takes Blake to finish a large

work means that, at the time of completion, the idea or insight that produced it may be that of a Blake long gone. This means, on the one hand, that he must be able to reanimate his own spirit of the past in order to carry on a work and, on the other, that he must still respect his older work to the extent, at the very least, that he will allow himself to be seen and judged in terms of it. Of course this view is consistent with his senses of tradition and continuity; it is the only one compatible with his working method but it is relatively rare among artists in such an extreme form. Although Blake has, of course, developed and matured as an artist and as a person, the chronological sequence of his works is much less important than it is for many others. A series of works can not be considered as developing or commenting on earlier works but is generally virtually independent. It is for this reason that the exhibition will be shown in thematic groups rather than in chronological sequence.

Blake will often have his models, in the form of photographic images, before him as he works and they not only allow him to take up work that he has left aside for some time but act in a general way like the studies of detail made by Renaissance painters; they may be combined in the same way. The process of drawing and then painting in glazes and scumbles does not generally leave an impenetrable, opaque surface in the flesh areas, rather it leaves a variety of marks of great diversity which can easily be distinguished by close inspection. They include lines (including traced lines), tones, shadows and local colours. There are also indications of change, of painting out, adjusting, rubbing down, reglazing and so on. It is always evident that the picture has been the result of much work and has been lived with for a considerable time. Although the images are compulsive and have a kind of certainty or inevitability, they never seem instantaneous. For this reason they have a look quite different from the pre-processed images of most Pop and Photo-realist artists.

* * *

The degree of incompletion in which Blake may leave his works and his practice of showing them or allowing them to be reproduced, sometimes several times in different stages of realisation, is closely associated with this exposure of his craft. It can be explained or illuminated in more than one way. As I have already suggested, it is a means of asserting that the ideal picture would take at least a whole lifetime, that he is continuing to work or even, that no image or idea can ever be quite complete. There is a charm in incompleteness that is deadened by perfection; a feeling that what is still growing is alive.

Blake also uses 'mistakes' in the same way. Early in this century when abstraction was being evolved, artists were careful to avoid a too perfect geometry in case it would deaden the art or reduce it to decoration. Blake aims at perfection but, I believe, takes pleasure in the picturesque qualities of imperfection. He may paint a 'perfect' mistake. It is possible to think of this feature as a declaration of independence from the photograph. I feel it also has some special unconscious meaning for Blake that has to do with the quality of fiction in his work that I have described. The reality of the painting must never quite destroy the sense that it is an illusion. I think that make-believe is important for him. It is in some way as necessary for his reality to be a fiction as for his fiction to be convincing.

Contrivances, like the illusion of incompleteness or damage, throughout Blake's work are the result of conscious adoption, in a consistent way, of devices that had been invented extempore for individual works. Blake aims at a reality without conventions but when they, necessarily, arise, he tries to make them visible and give them a rationale.

There is also one special type of incompleteness that I think must be more important than its technical explanation may suggest. This is the fact that he will often leave one eye unfinished while the other stares out clearly at the viewer. Many pictures have been shown in this condition and that it is not altogether accidental seems to be demonstrated by the cases where one eye has been obliterated. In the early 'Children Reading Comics' (Cat. no. 4) the girl is wearing an eyepatch as does the later Conrad in the 'Da Vinci Brothers' (Cat. no. 54). 'Loelia' (Cat. no. 21) has a 'damaged' eye and in 'Siriol' (Cat. no. 22) and 'Irish Lord X' (Cat. no. 53) it has been 'vandalised'. In 'Dixie' (Cat. no. 24) the illusory split in the panel runs through her eye. 'Bo Diddley' (Cat. no. 50) and 'Aparicio' (Cat. no. 75) each have an eye in dark shadow and the recent 'Fairy Child Crying' (Cat. no. 93) has an eye quite invisible in the shadow. So I think it cannot have been an accident that two versions of Titania have been shown in a transitional state with one very complete eye and the other looking incomplete or blind. I cannot give it a meaning that the artist would recognise but, for me, this curious feature seems to point to two contradictory themes. One is the unblinking, all-seeing eye of the mythical Cyclops or the single, shared eye of the Graeae. The other is that it might be inhibiting to be watched by two such highly realised eyes while one was scrutinising the rest of the body. There is a strange analogy in the work 'Window' (Cat. no. 41) where one is led to peer into the simulated room only to be caught out prying by the dummy head looming so close. For Blake, however, one eye is enough to characterise the head sufficiently for the figure to progress and the other can wait until the whole is to be finished.

Another feature of Blake's painting, closely related to the unfinished look, is the damaged look. This is particularly a part of the circus women ('Siriol', 'Loelia', 'Dixie') but appears in many of the accompanying figures of the series of wrestlers, especially the one at the top of 'Doktor Tortur' (Cat. no. 57). 'Kid McCoy' (Cat. no. 58) was also deliberately 'distressed'. Blake sometimes paints in brown colours that suggest old paint which has sunk, darkened or even flaked off and been retouched. Such signs of age, wear and damage are clearly deliberate imperfections but seem to me to be marks of affection as well. Things we have possessed and lived with get damaged. The damage is caused by their use and we do not throw them away if we love them. One of the charms of Blake's work is that it looks lived with in the same way.

All these marks of the artist's presence are essential to the pictures in which they are found. In some cases they give the impression that there was a separate Peter Blake who made a series of works. The author of the early pictures is young and boyish, shy but keen to show off himself, his friends and his possessions. The author of the circus paintings is older, perhaps a circus person himself, naif and enthusiastic, proud of his skill in fairground baroque lettering. His women are rather old fashioned and look experienced in their glitter. The 'circus artist's' works appeared in the middle of the 'boy artist's' period and so, in this period, the artist was painting as two rather different persona.

Later on come paintings or collages fictionally by the fans of pop stars, movie stars and wrestling. The authors of the wrestlers seem more expert, perhaps older than the boys or girls who idolise Elvis and Kim Novak. In fact it is possible to discern two artists for each of these pictures. The collector who I have just described and the poster artist who has done the figures and lettering. The Ruralist painter of Alice, Ophelia and fairies is again a very different artist. Of course they are all Peter Blake – aspects of his own character and tastes. I think some are close to the real, whole Peter Blake and some are assumed personalities conjured out of himself. The nearest analogy is with the way a writer creates an author for a novel written in the first person, one who is not quite himself but must be part of himself. Such a role may be lived out in all sincerity by Blake himself and is always partly so. He is a collector of objects like the circus figures, a fan of wrestling and belonged to the Brotherhood of Ruralists. I think this fact is the converse of his way of giving truth to a character by inventing a plausible history. The painter has to be equally convincing. The works which are most real, which inhabit real space and need the fewest accessories, are the figures of the Ruralist and more recent periods, during which the role of the painter and his life have been most closely integrated.

* * *

The pictures of wrestlers (Cat.nos.52–65) are the type of the synthetic or composite work. They show the device of creating character by accumulating attributes at its clearest. They are, however, a development from what went before. The idea goes back to the pictures of children and the self portrait with badges. The boys show their interests and define themselves by the objects they collect, by their clothes, ties and badges. There is an extra element of fantasy in 'On the Balcony' (Cat.no.15) where they hold little paintings in the style of Blake's contemporaries at the Royal College and by his brother. What children would choose such things if they were not going to be Peter Blake?

In these works some of the attributes, which are like those of saints in religious painting, are executed in the same painterly illusion as the rest of the picture. Others are painted heraldically and may be in glossier paint so that they stand out as objects. The 'Drum Majorette' (Cat.no.26), derived partly from the style of the American cartoonist Saul Steinberg who often used the device of combining different stylistic realities in one drawing, wears a real pair of dark glasses. The medals are individual objects that Blake collected to resemble medals and so they stand outside the illusion. The circus ladies, like 'Loelia' (Cat.no. 21), had their 'attributes' tattooed on their bodies: old and new images suggesting their family, their history and their dream boyfriends. Here again the iconic convention allows the images to lie on the surface of the painting, unaffected by perspective or modelling. They have real costume jewellery on their dress.

The mature format of the wrestlers is that of a kind of homely shrine. Although it resembles to some extent both an icon and the kind of arrangement a person may make on a chimney piece or side table, it is an invention of Blake's own; it is fiction like the characters to whom it is dedicated. The pictures are framed and usually divided into panels by simple black fillets. One panel will contain a portrait, conceived more or less as a poster. The name will be written in sign writing in a style that matches the character. 'Little Lady Luck' (Cat. no. 59), for example, is written in rainbow colours referring to the mythical pot of gold to be found at the end of the rainbow. There are often plain, decorative panels which may be painted in gloss paint like doors, signs or furniture and there are generally little badges, charms or toys that stand for memorabilia or possessions. A fictional wrestler may start from just such an element and have attributes before Blake has found the body, face and hair style to go with them. In one case, 'The Masked Zebra Kid' (Cat. no. 55), the wrestler was a real one. The attributes include his actual signature and a toy zebra, also a real mask concealing the face. One does not know whether there is a painted face or only a ghastly void behind it.

Some of these attributes are carefully placed in time. 'Roxy Roxy' (Cat. no. 62) was conceived as being of the 1940s and 1950s, rather straight and very English, on a tour to the U.S.A. Later she became more patriotic and Tory. The spirit of the character is conveyed by badges. The ship on which she is imagined to have sailed to America, the *Aquitania*, is at the top of the frame as a souvenir and in it as a postcard she might have sent to her parents. However the imaginary compiler's sense of history is not too secure and anachronisms occur. The ship and some of the badges are too early and the hair-style, while 'conservative' in spirit, is too late.

The use of attributes and collected items to characterise the subject of a painting extends to quite different types of work. I have already mentioned the tattooing of the circus ladies and the badges and wrestling paintings. It is clear that such a work as 'Toy Shop' (Cat. no. 37) is the stock of a fictional shop owner whom you might see if you were to open the door. He is rather old-fashioned and has kept some lines that a shopkeeper obsessed by turnover would have taken out of the window long ago. The objects are stylistically heterogeneous but all are cheap and homely. All of us will remember having prized their like when we were young and will search the window for the momentos of our own past. The shopkeeper is to that extent an everyman and his shop a museum – in fact, Blake's own. If some items are foreign-made they have been domesticised. It is a little difficult now, after twenty years of Portobello Road, and in a period when the word 'collectables' comprises almost the whole range of objects more than five years old, to recollect the novelty of this work when it first appeared in 1962. The striking thing about it and about Blake's work generally was that it did not imply that the creator of it and its 'consumers' were equally and highly sophisticated or 'trendy' in either the high arts or the American popular arts. Everything suggests the context of the British high street and home.

* * *

I have tried to explain above how Blake builds up a composite character by elements of dress, style, name, lettering, frame and the assemblage of associative or evocative objects. The power of such assemblages depends on Blake's ability to bring into play associations which, though differing from viewer to viewer, are there to be evoked in the minds of many people. Images may include not only the faces and names of famous people but elements analogous to those used by real wrestlers to build up a character, which I have referred to. That is, he uses body types and poses, face types, name, literary types and, of course, ethnic and sex types.

In a world that has become acutely conscious of prejudice based on cultural stereotypes of race and sex it is difficult to characterise adequately and dispassionately Blake's use of such stereotypes. They are the elements of a kind of fiction which can be recognised as fantasy that is 'untrue' but is, nevertheless, a means of expressing his true affections and can in turn be recognised by his public. Blake's affections extend to the ugly and distorted as well as to the beautiful and symmetrical, to black as well as white, to old and young, male and female, to the childish and the sophisticated. The combinations old or black with ugly do not, in Blake's painting, connote 'old is ugly' or 'black is ugly' and by extension 'bad', because both are 'good' and equally relished by Blake. But they need to be discernible in order to function and Blake, like other figurative artists, is bound to start from that point. His affection can be seen in the way he treats his characters; in, for example, the care with which he realises them.

An instance which we can begin to analyse is the wrestling picture of 'The Da Vinci Brothers' (Cat. no. 54). The basic elements that go to make up this fictional tag team are mostly quite obvious. They are first the idea of a tag team, that is a pair of wrestlers only one of whom should be in the ring at any moment. Nearly always both are goodies or both baddies but they are distinguished from one another by other characteristics. Here both are villains, one is bald and rather brutal; the other affects the air and style of an 'English Gentleman'. In such a context to be a gentleman is itself suspect but this act is intended to be obviously false. The man is too Italian, too rugged and handsome, he has an implausible, too ambitious name, 'da Vinci',

and a Germanic first name, 'Conrad', as well as a false title. He is wearing a hunting stock with a blazer decorated by a gothic but tawdry initial. Above all he is wearing an eye-patch – a sure sign of a 'villain'. The relatively crude fairground lettering itself implies that all is an illusion. In fact the fictional character of the work, itself betrayed by little fictional mistakes, can be taken to illustrate the falsity of stereotypes and others like them which, however, exist by virtue of a consensus.

*   *   *

There is another sense in which Blake's work may be composite. This is his use of more than one photographic source to build up a figure. It may be a means of acquitting himself of copying (which is quite unnecessary because all such images are entirely transformed in the painting) but it is something more. In 'La Petite Reine Africaine' (Cat. no. 64) the lower part of the face is drawn from a news photograph of a black man, his mouth half open showing irregular teeth, the upper part, including the hair, is drawn from a cosmetic advertisement in a women's magazine, the body and the outline of the head from a third source. The head of Puck (Cat. no. 83) has the face of the Pop music personality Del Shannon, superimposed on the head and body of a young boy.

In these cases and others the details of the face are older and more heavily marked than the bodies would lead us to expect. The effect is partly the same as that of the early pictures, where the process of correction and refinement of the features has caused them to expand within the outline of the face. They are more expressive than those of pretty children and the doll-like women of many advertisements. I think Blake has a particular feeling of affection for people whose faces show the signs, even the damage, of experience. But here there is a piquancy in the combination of innocence or naivety with knowingness, sometimes sexiness. Many of Blake's figures of women and boys are drawn with open mouths and with lips that are slightly lined or creased and wet, they may even appear slightly bruised. Such a face is 'Blanche Neige' (Cat. no. 65), another fictional tag wrestler. Here the eyes, nose and mouth are all slightly too large for the outlines of the face and the effect is to turn the girl into a kind of elf, staring at the viewer and, with mock innocence, exposing her keenness and wish to please. Her hair lying close to her head and the pallor of her skin suggest the pathos and the androgynous type of the pierrot.

Comparing the existing work with a photograph of it at an earlier stage (illustrated with Cat. no. 65), you can see that one of Blake's favourite facial outlines has been very subtly mitigated in the completed work. As shown at the Waddington Gallery in 1977 (no. 58), the face had a rather narrow brow but was wider across the cheek bone and hinge of the jaw, developing into a perfectly curved outline of the lower jaw and chin. The shape is related to Blake's own face type and, again, is a tradition for representing elves or gnomes which brings together attributes of childhood with those of age to produce an effect of agelessness. I cannot easily produce a pedigree for this image but it may owe something to the Flemish masters of the Renaissance, Bosch and Brueghel; it descends through Dadd, Tenniel, Rackham and Maxfield Parrish (who used his own male, mature body as the model for girls and children). Certainly our culture's concept of the fairy or elf combines elements of childhood and smallness, but also of great age or agelessness, unconventional beauty or ugliness

and so on.

In the finished version of 'Blanche Neige and Bet Noir' the configuration is made less conspicuous by enlarging the outline of the hair and bringing it down the temples. The elf-like look is merely an undertone in a visage which has become rather more brash. The pallor of the skin is also diminished while the pathos of the one-eyed 'Bet' in the same picture has been almost transformed into animal aggression with two staring eyes.

*　*　*

The frontal, virtually symmetrical figure which appears twice over in this picture, is a recurring feature in Blake's art. His self-portraits and early children are examples but recently most of the cases are female. They begin with the circus figures in their bras and g-strings, reappear as topless wrestlers and have their most powerful incarnation as fairies – 'Titania' (Cat. no. 85) and the Ruralist 'Definitive Nude' (Cat. no. 98a). The pose is finally that of an Egyptian God or Greek kouros. Blake does not recognise these sources, he thinks rather of a person posing for a snapshot. This is to me an instance of that which seems simply natural to Blake corresponding to a timeless archetype and may account in part for the magic of his best work. I think the circus ladies, the female wrestlers, the strippers and nude figures formed a series of beauty types and nude figures, each seen through the eyes of a different Peter Blake.

Clearly one of the recurrent themes of Blake's work is the continuity of childhood in maturity. It has already been referred to in several places in this introduction and could be mentioned in relation to almost every characteristic that one may attempt to pick out and describe. It is important,

[23]

I think, to stress the element of maturity, even sophistication, that is an essential part of it. Looking back, it is remarkable that a young artist in his teens and twenties experiencing a period as a clerk in the R.A.F. and then studying at the Royal College, should have chosen to depict boys and girls of ten or twelve. He was at an age when most of us are determined to forget or suppress our pre-adolescent selves. Blake was secure enough not only to paint children but to identify himself with them (Cat. nos. 7a–7b).

The subjects are often transformations of himself or family. They may be taken from family snapshots of the kind that are an embarrassment to many young adults who can remember the agony of having to pose for them. The pictures, as I have said, celebrate juvenile enthusiasms, the Saturday film club or weekly comics. The style of painting, slightly primitive with oval faces, low foreheads and heads disproportionately large, is one that is related to what is an almost universal children's style. Children, when they paint, tend to enlarge the important features, whether faces or the objects in the picture that give it its theme. Blake's space, which allows every object its real size, undiminished by perspective, is related to the kind of space often found in their paintings as is his tendency to allow a pattern to emerge and to spread over the surface of the painting. But these 'child-like' features in the art are also tokens of a kind of sophistication. Blake's obvious painterly skill shows that he is capable of 'correct' perspective; he is creating a partial illusion of childishness by means of a mature skill. He is able to look dispassionately at his own younger self.

The pictures of boys and girls contain, even within the fiction they illustrate, the theme of maturity in childhood. The badges, for example, refer in various ways to the attempts of the little boys to grow up. Joining a film club 'ABC Minors' (Cat. no. 7b) is a way of associating with a group outside the family. Other badges refer to politicians and people who, we must imagine, the children do not know much about but who, for them, belong to the outer world of adults. Dark glasses were an adult mode. Several of the little boys wear hand-painted ties of beauty queens. Blake himself wore such ties painted by himself but at a rather older age. He is attributing to the boys a slightly precocious, and perhaps naif, sexuality.

The piquancy of the idea of juvenile and adolescent sexuality is something that is fairly universally felt in our culture and, since the publication of Nabokov's novel *Lolita*, has been represented much more explicitly than it was in the mid 1950s. Blake expressed it in these pictures in a half ironic way and by means that were only just beyond what would have been considered at the time normal. That the irony is conscious is made clear to the viewer in little jokes. One of the ties portrays 'Miss C.W.S'. She is the beauty queen of the Co-op, an organisation which, at that date at least, was the least likely to elect a girl to such a title. This detail is at the same time a reference to the fact that the C.W.S. seemed to supply and arrange everything in Dartford; it was the dominant social and political institution. Blake is saying 'that was my world' in a way that he knew would be understood by relatively few people in the art world. He is showing that he is a member of one of the infinity of social groups or subcultures which have their own proud and knowledgeable members, but whose signs and conventions may be beyond the viewer's ken.

Blake's fairy idiom is, in its way, one that is

strongly associated with childhood and permits, by a convention existing in our culture, a mixing of childish and adult elements. It is not a very ancient convention. It goes back to the mid-nineteenth century, but not to the distant past of folk-tale and celtic myth, and has been taken over and transformed by Blake himself. His fairies are generally either boys or girls, during or soon after the age of puberty. The convention is that fairies do not wear human clothes and may decorate their bodies in a way that is free of the human inhibitions that are associated with dress and undress. Blake knows, of course, that cultures which require the wearing of clothes, at least our western one, take a peculiar interest in unconscious nudity and that this is associated with a supposed innocence and thus with childhood. There is no doubt that his work appeals directly to this taste and deliberately so. He is himself not innocent in the sense of ignorant but, although he may paint this kind of innocence, his work is, on the contrary, sanctioned by its sophistication which is partly communicated by devices such as the strengthening and ageing of the features, described above.

The theme is not parodied to the extent that it is either repudiated or loses its force but the degree of irony, which is conveyed in a style that always remains visibly artificial, sees to it that the work is distanced. The most obvious irony is conveyed in the choice of the fairy as a convention, for Blake can rely on an audience which does not 'believe in' fairies so that every element of plausibility, including the degree to which the particular eroticism plays upon desire, only accentuates the force of that irony. This is another instance of Blake's magic, his ability to convince you simultaneously that 'it is true' and 'it is not true'. Blake also recognises that fairies are unacceptable in the world of modern art; they are a gesture of defiance to it and he is not afraid to take them seriously.

* * *

The subjects of Blake's works include both High Art and popular art: both may be quoted or referred to. Such quotations evolve almost imperceptibly from the graphic art he had made as a student at Gravesend.

An early drawing and the lithograph made from it (Cat. no. 183) show two ladies gossiping in front of a shop window. The window contains objects and lettering which suggest the context of the women's lives just as the attributes of the wrestlers were to do. The shop window and door are plainly the prototype of the 'Toy Shop' and 'Doors' (Cat. nos. 37 and 36, 39). Similarly, another drawing shows a table top from above, its edge and a chequered tablecloth below, a formula which was converted into the Pop art works with their dividing battens and the heraldic stripes or chevrons below which suggest the hard-edge abstraction that was contemporary with Pop and shared some of its compositional devices. An archery target, larger than the air-gun targets of the 'Toy Shop', is simply collaged on to the surface of 'The First Real Target' which therefore distinguishes itself from the painted targets of Jasper Johns. Blake even painted what looks like a conceptual work, 'Come Stanley' (Cat. no. 40). However this is really a very laconic work of Pop art. It is a reconstruction of a frame of a silent movie giving the catch phrase of Oliver Hardy addressed to Stanley Laurel. This is a refined descendant of the phrases in balloons that he had included in pastiches of comics in the student magazine, *Ark*, while at the Royal College. It is typical of Blake both that the phrase could only be recognised by a person who was familiar with Laurel and Hardy films, not then so much a cult of the intelligentsia as now, and that, having done it, he should be satisfied not to repeat the idea. The same is true of the reference to Johns above.

Modern art appeared first as a subject in the pictures held by the children in 'On the Balcony' which represent the work of Blake's contemporaries, Robyn Denny, Dick Smith and Leon Kossoff as well as Blake's own brother. The reference in this painting is to a large work by the American Social Realist, Honore Sharrer, whose picture 'Workers and their Paintings' in the Museum of Modern Art shows workers holding masterpieces of modern painting. In this work, obviously there is a suggestion that the poor have the same right to art as the rich. Blake's work says the same thing but in a different way.

Blake's work contained, as I have mentioned, certain references to Pop art as practised in America and Britain but it was also considered to be Pop art itself and there are groups of works which he, himself, refers to as 'Pop art'. This means, in effect, that his subject matter was analogous to that of certain Pop artists or, like 'The First Real Target' (Cat.no.33), commented on it.

A part of the concept of Pop art, as formulated in the Independent Group at the ICA in the mid 1950s, was the 'fine art–pop art continuum'. In this sense 'pop art' refers not to paintings but to what became the source materials: comics, publicity stills, advertising, packaging etc. On the one hand, this represented a quasi anthropological view of one's own culture and, on the other, it was both the open manifestation of a critical attack on the snobbism of the high art sub-culture and a celebration of working class and lower middle class taste. Generally no positive attitude was taken to academic art and, except in the first year or two, little attention paid to British artefacts. Blake needed no theoretical backing to take a similar view but his range did extend to these less blatant and exotic creations. His training in graphic art provided the beginnings of a technique adequate to work anywhere in the field and his own tastes were not exclusive.

The pop–fine art continuum is manifested in several ways in Blake's work, as the allusions described above demonstrate. It shows equally in the relationship of his style or styles to the contents of works. From an early date he has painted different elements in different ways. He has used traditional techniques, adapted from the practice of painting from life, working from a flat-work model such as a photograph or printed reproduction. That is, he has used a fine art style to represent a popular art image. He has also inserted into his pictures elements like badges, either painted or collaged, words or numbers may be painted in a signwriter's style, be assembled out of stock letters, be handwritten or appear integrated as part of the thing seen. He sometimes imitates characteristic mistakes of the mass media as in the fringe effect in 'Bo Diddley' (Cat.no.50).

Blake's 'Sculpture Park', together with the 'Incidents from a Sculpture Park' on a larger scale (Cat.no.137), comprise his most elaborate comment on modern art. It is conceived as a model park in which are set-out found and constructed objects that resemble well known sculpture styles. Each has its group of viewers, a theme recalling Henry Moore's well known drawing 'Crowd Looking at a Tied up Object'. Many of the figures are naturalistic, modified plastic or metal scale-models of soldiers, cowboys and other types.

These may crowd around a stylised sculpture but in some cases the figures of the viewers are themselves stylised as sculptures while the sculpture is in another convention. There are set pieces in which a whole group refers to the style of an individual artist. The irony which pervades the work is certainly only visible to those who can recognise the styles and, at the most obvious level, the work is a good humoured, but still pointed, satire on modernism. However, Blake recognises that modern art raises many problems of reality, representation, skill, expression and so on which have their parallels in toys, models and even cartoons.

Accordingly, his references include on the one hand, accidental resemblances of a natural or man-made object, such as a toy, to a work of art, and on the other hand, reference to the physical and psychological resources of artists. The use of toys is itself a reference to the quotation of popular images in Pop art. The stones from which Moore sometimes takes his inspiration are represented by actual pebbles. A single squashed toy car represents the compressed car-body work of the American John Chamberlain and the French César. Obviously the resemblance of the toy car to the real one (more conceptual than visual) is paralleled in the resemblance of toy sculpture to the real ones. The self-imposed heroism of Stuart Brisley is depicted by a toy which, itself, takes its image from heroic prototypes of cartoon and film. The slick neatness of the toy contrasts with the deliberate repulsiveness of many of the actions performed by the artist.

The range of the works represented or referred to in Blake's sculptures goes beyond contemporary art and includes (just as Warhol quoted the 'Mona Lisa') high art images that have been popular icons like the 'Venus de Milo' and all kinds of visual stereotypes and imitations like the cottages along the road.

* * *

There are distinct and intentional variations in scale within and between the Park and the sample Parks. Scale has been a significant element in Blake's practice. In early works like the 'Love Wall' (Cat.no.36) in which he collaged images from magazines, the scale of images varied in relation to space available or to the importance attached to them, just as it does in the magazines themselves and in the 'media environment', referred to by Pop theoreticians. It is a feature of photography, the reprographic processes and layout. Works like 'On the Balcony' are built on a wide variation of image sizes in the quoted pictures, whether badges, magazines or packaging, which is contrasted with the non-diminishing perspective of the real space. In 'The Knife Thrower's board' (Cat.no.25) he had made use of an image whose cult following responded to the fact that it was a life-size Brigitte Bardot unfolding from the tabloid.

Among Blake's later works, many heads are shown staring out of a constricting canvas, panel or frame, so that they remind one of the image in a pocket mirror like some make-up advertisements. The scale seems to bring the heads close, both physically and psychologically. The faces, too, are so close that they inhibit a close inspection, a fact intensified by the prominence of the kind of detail often avoided by generalising photographers and painters, like the lined lips and sometimes, the irregular teeth behind them. The slight enlargement of features in proportion to faces, that I have mentioned, is often echoed in the enlargement of heads in relation to bodies. Blake had been taught at Gravesend to draw the head either large or small in relation to the body. He more often chose the former since, of course, the head is for him the most expressive feature but it also has the effect of suggesting the proportions of a child.

In the sculpture parks the scale is varied so that the same figure may appear on several scales, as it may in the wrestlers series, but systematically. The variations are partly opportunistic, in that some images may have been found only in a size which may then determine that of the watchers but I think it also relates to the ratio of the size of a representation to the amount of detail that can be accommodated or perceived. This is a basic limit in Blake's own concept of the completion. The lower limit of brush stroke sizes determines the resolution of the image so that, just as in microscopy, the degree of precision is proportional to the scale. On the other hand there is a magic in the tiny but precise representation of a thing which seems to fascinate children of a certain age who, when younger, had been able to associate dolls and toys together according to morphological type, regardless of scale.

In the 'Sculpture Park' the space is naturally three-dimensional but Blake has used a number of different conventions to represent the space in which his figures live. Some early works, like the drawing (Cat. no. 183), are presumably in perspective but the rear plane is filled by a vertical construction, in this case apparently the window of a shop. There is no ground plan and no recessive lines of significance. The device of such a plane is repeated in the 'Self Portrait with Badges' (Cat. no. 19), in the form of a fence, but here there are the half-realised details of a frontstage and gaps which give glimpses of a garden beyond but,

again, there is no defined deep space.

Some of the larger works of the late 1950s and early 1960s represent both the ground plane and vertical plane by means of the vertical dimension. The convention is that of an unusual axonometric, but there are discrepancies. 'On the Balcony' is the most complete manifestation. The road and pavement as well as the side-views of objects are drawn vertically and without recession. Some of the quoted images hang in the same plane but other objects (the largest of which is the painter's table in the middle distance) are twisted into free isometric parallelograms. Small objects lying on the ground may also be twisted to show that they are scattered. There is very little overlapping except where it is a conscious dramatic feature, for example in the boy covering his face with a mask from *Life Magazine*.

In the meantime some of the smaller works, such as 'Boy with New Tie' (Cat. no. 139), use a convention which is related to the Madonna paintings of the fifteenth century. The figure in half-length fills the foreground but there is a horizon, decorated with feathery trees, appearing on either side. The space between foreground and background is not marked, so that the landscape element appears as a backdrop. The circus ladies are again icons with no depicted ambient space. The lettering, however, may be painted in a conventional three-dimensional illusion. The wrestlers and their like generally inhabit a neutral space like that of some fifteenth- and sixteenth-century portraits especially the late Holbeins. A plain field of colour lies behind the head whose richness and luminosity implies a kind of depth just as velvet does.

Some of the portraits and, especially, the Hollywood paintings (Cat. nos. 104–106) have a 'legitimate' perspective equivalent to that of a photograph. These are quite rare in Blake's painting in that two of them have a wide angle of vision and compose several figures together in an almost equal manner. Blake's vertical perspective had been 'correct' for his children: now a photographic space is 'correct' for Los Angeles. Between these works there lie the 'Postcards' (Cat. nos. 72–77) and the collaged works. In the latter the space is often real; that of panels, mouldings, etc. framing the variously focused photographic illusions. In other cases the carpentry is painted in *trompe l'oeil*. In the 'Postcards' the photographic space is simulated and the panel or canvas becomes the paper.

There are other kinds of spatial illusions in the doors (Cat. nos. 36–37) and windows (Cat. no. 41). Here there are real spaces inside the windows and virtual space too – reflections of the viewer himself in the glass or shiny panel. The viewer sees himself among the stars or in the world of make believe and nostalgia. There is also the fantasy space of the rooms to which the doors and windows lead. It is a space half-revealed, another world into which one may be lucky enough to penetrate.

The space of the fairies, because it is so convincing, is a space into which one may be half tempted to intrude, although its inhabitants often seem to stare one out rather rudely. It is like that of storybook illustrations and the ambience depends entirely on the main figures. Other figures float or peer through leaves or branches. Because they are of uncertain size they are of uncertain distance so the space is that of dream or magic.

* * *

One thing I have not sufficiently discussed is the hand-writing, that is, the characteristic brushwork in Blake's painting. One of the reasons he may leave a picture unfinished or hesitate to complete it is, simply, that he enjoys the visible brush strokes that will disappear or become almost completely integrated in the finished work. They are certainly one of the most enjoyable features of it. They are of a number of kinds, indeed of such a great number that I could not enumerate them even if there were words adequate to describe and distinguish them. They are the tools of the trade of a great craftsman but one who works in such a way that the result seems always to be at risk until the final moment.

They include at least the following. First there are those that are directly mimetic either of details, like hairs, or of artificial elements, like lettering. In the latter case it may be that the imitation is not so much of an appearance as of a manner of painting such as housepainting or sign-writing. Then, one may occasionally see the remains of the outlines of forms, of shadows or highlights traced directly or by means of the epidiascope. There are also visual devices that are to a degree mimetic but which correspond to the conventions of historic painting, local colour, shading, etc. There are brush marks, like those of Rubens or Rembrandt (to name the greatest), whose function is to animate and give character to the surface. Some of these are adjusted subsequently by, for example, rubbing down, which may thin and texture them, fray them out, let lower layers show through or leave almost imperceptible discontinuities to the surface skin as if irregular patches of paint had flaked off. This is not the only example of Blake producing an effect like that of age and accident to a painting. There are many passages that resemble wear, overcleaning, the revealing of underpainting and corrections (*pentimenti*), darkening or sinking of paint etc. In some cases, as I have mentioned, he actually distresses or fakes damage to the painting.

However there are other marks of the brush that are intrinsic to the way he realises an image. In his drawings one may see how one area or object in the picture is realised in detail as a vignette, with hatching and other broad marks to create tone or shade, the rest being indicated by a few simple outlines. In his oil paintings one may see outlines which have been painted over, some in ink and others marked by a traced point. Such lines are very extended, slightly irregular but confident. They do not show signs of constant correction although, in drawings, you may see a line progressing two steps forward and two back in an oblique, saw-tooth rhythm, as in 'Props from Cleopatra'. Where it occurs, such an outline indicates a form more or less directly derived from nature or photographs. In drawings and watercolours the final form is generally closed by such a line whether it was in fact drawn in first or not. Certainly, in the case of drawings, there are rarely areas of tone without outline so that the implication is that the outline precedes the tone. In paintings this may also be the case but in certain instances an outline may be used to redefine what has previously been an indefinite, sometimes even incoherent, scumble that may blot out a previous outline. Blake is fond of quoting an early teacher: 'When in doubt put a black line around it'. More often, the form breaks out of the line which remains as an alternate image, the archaeological residue of a mutating reality or, simply, an element in the texture of the whole.

More generally the process, as I have described it, is from indeterminacy, characterised by very free brush strokes, to determinacy, characterised by fine or smooth strokes. Although this distinction may seem obvious it is not by any means universally the rule and there have been other artists who create a precise if not complete passage from the start.

After a pale, translucent scumble, Blake adds stronger glazes and scumbles that occupy the positions of the limbs or parts of the body to be painted. These more violent marks may run along the axis of the form, suggesting sometimes main areas of highlight or shadow and, sometimes, although not I think intentionally, the lines of structural elements: bones and muscles. Other marks loop round or zig-zag across the forms. The effect is very frequently one of movement or of disintegration and curiously similar to certain passages in the highly charged work of painters like de Kooning and Francis Bacon. So, when the paintings are exhibited in this condition, it may be difficult to read marks of this type simply as rough approximations to forms. Equally, in those areas which are left transparent because the scumble that establishes the surface has not been added, it is tempting to read them as the arrested incarnation or disintegration of the body. Similarly there are spots, blots, hard and soft edges where paint has suffused and dyed the submerged layers in his water colours that, on very close inspection, have the appearance of decay, yet, at the proper distance they go to make up the immense complexity and therefore the vitality of the surface. I think, for Blake, they are the marks of his delight in the power of painting to conjure up visions by magic, just as the unexpected juxtaposition of elements is an expression of his delight in the power to make anything happen.

A final glaze or very thin scumble may be laid over a whole figure or complex area of painting to unify it. Even then Blake's resources have not run out. He knows for example how to polish the paint of a strong blue sky with the palm of his hand so as to give it light. His works show every sign of a man who loves painting.

*   *   *

There is no artist in the world remotely like Peter Blake. His individuality, however, is not due to insularity, though no one could be more British, nor is it due to any kind of impenetrable self-preoccupation, for his themes can be recognised everywhere and in the hearts of many of us. Still less is it due to any primitivism or lack of culture, for Blake is highly skilled and very much at home in many of the cultures that make up our complex society. On the contrary, it is the outcome of national characteristics, of interests, skills and culture that he does share with others but in a degree and in a mixture that is strong enough to make his voice heard across most of the boundaries of nation, culture and even age.

He has said that the purchaser of one of his paintings will have at least a lot of work. But Blake offers much more than this. He has been in the habit of trying to add a bonus to each painting, something extra: in the 'Toy Shop', electric light and an abundance of objects; in 'Got a Girl', a record to be played; in 'Come Stanley', the opportunity for each of us to remember our favourite Laurel and Hardy disaster. More integrally we have the chance to 'see the painter at work' when he exhibits unfinished pictures. However, there is always a more important free gift attached to a Blake painting. It is the magic with which he can conjure up and realise all kinds of things which we will never find in real life. That is Blake's work.

Michael Compton

PETER BLAKE & THE RURALISTS

A ruralist as defined in the dictionary is quite simply 'someone from the city who moves to the country'. Peter Blake, with his now ex-wife Jann Haworth and first child Liberty, became a ruralist when, in 1969, he left London and went to live in a former railway station at Wellow near Bath. Six years later he became a Ruralist (with a capital R), when, after conversations with David Inshaw and later Graham Arnold, painters both living and working nearby in Devizes, a spontaneous decision was made to form the Brotherhood of Ruralists.

Now, eight years on, Peter Blake is once again firmly established in London. The Brotherhood is showing, perhaps for the last time together as a formal group, six uniformly sized nude paintings, known among themselves, in the same half-humorous, half-serious sense they christened themselves the Ruralists, as the 'Definitive Nude'.

Their appearance here is at Peter Blake's insistence. Though unorthodox style for a major one-man retrospective of this kind, it is revealing of the man and the importance to him and his art of the past decade or so of 'being in the country', the artistic friendships he made there and the immense impact of all this on the direction his work has taken.

The word 'Ruralist' was chosen because, as Peter Blake once remarked, it was 'more to do with the fact that we were all in the country. It was not quite that much about the land, it was about being in the country.' In this sense Peter Blake regarded himself, if unconsciously, as a ruralist from the moment the decision was made to leave London to go down and live in Wellow. For immediately he made the move, he became as assiduous a participant in and observer of the myths and legends of country life as he had formerly been of urban life and culture during the sub-American 1950s and swinging British 1960s.

The reasons for making that decision, like most personal decisions, will never really be known; disillusionment with the silly fag-end of the late 1960s culture, the move to the West Country of other close painter friends of his generation, Joe Tilson, Howard Hodgkin and Richard Smith in particular, and the birth of their first child a year before. In a curious way the reason for the decision is rather less important than the fact that it happened. For, once there, Peter Blake, unlike most of his distinguished painter contemporaries, whose move to the country made little discernible impact on their work, could not help but join in the new country life wholeheartedly both as a painter and person. In artistic terms the catalyst between this new life and his painting was, as it had been so often for him in the past, the idea of childhood and youth.

Now, however, it was given a quite new relevance by the fact that it was not arrived at simply through the filter of his own childhood myth but through the direct experience of his young children. Woven into this was a growing fascination with the work of the great Victorian children's writers and illustrators, of whom he and Jann had started collecting examples in the mid-1960s with the enthusiastic support of the painter Graham Ovenden, a recent student of his at the Royal College of Art and an early and passionately knowledgeable student of Victorian culture.

Out of his children's experience came the startling realisation that these writers and illustrators possessed an extraordinarily sensitive, almost peculiar, gift for entering into and understanding the emotional and imaginative world of a child. Of them all, undoubtedly the most important for him was Lewis Carroll and it was on Alice that the first fruits of 'being in the country' found their principal focus. The now classic sequence of eight Alice watercolours, later also published as prints, have deservedly become among the best known and most popular works he has ever done, possessing much of the same quality as Tenniel's original illustrations in their ability to combine literal realism with the wild imaginative leaps of children's logic in a way that matches so perfectly the spirit of the text. Moreover the topiary hedges and gardens that provide their setting and are such a vital part of their claustrophobic imagery, and of Carroll's writing, are quite new to Peter Blake's painting. They are unthinkable without the move to the country and to Wellow in particular, a village with a peculiarly cut-off and isolated feeling tucked away in one of those secluded valleys so characteristic of the countryside south of Bath. Lewis Carroll was to occupy many of the aspects of the life he and Jann created in their railway station – the making of a garden based on the Alice chess-game and incorporating other 'Alice' quotations, and in 1973 the foundation of a small school in the village, christened the Looking-Glass School, which was to pioneer highly imaginative child-based teaching methods.

Another very strong element in Peter Blake's growing fascination with the Victorian imagination, both visual and verbal, was his recognition of the passion and delight in 'telling a story' that he shared intuitively with it. Perhaps the commonest and most misleading misapprehension of Victorian art and design is to label such attitudes as literary. There is, as Peter Blake recognised instantly, a world of difference between the two. For whether it was mural schemes, furniture design or book illustration, there was, in the Victorians, a general and total obsession with depicting everything, and a compelling urge to present a visual story to the spectator that was as complete and entire in what it included as possible; literal perhaps, but not literary. Hence the obsession with detail and with technique that are its chief characteristics. It is so often at its greatest when applied to the re-creation of a past age of myth, poetry and legend and in the realms of fantasy, where it re-creates literally and with compelling conviction. Such methods made the Victorians, among other things, powerful illus-

trators able to invent powerful visual worlds standing parallel but not subservient to their verbal sources.

The importance of technique to them has much to do with Peter Blake's increasing awareness of his own working methods, in particular his move from acrylic paint with its flat, bland surfaces back to the greater flexibility of oil applied with fine sable brushes. A growing interest in this technique reached its apogee in 'Titania', begun in 1976 after the formation of the Brotherhood. The choice of the fairy subject matter though drawn from Shakespeare, also has much more to do with the Victorian painters' and writers' fascination with Shakespeare's fairy imagery than with a particular interest in Shakespeare.

Before looking at this and his other later 1970s paintings however, it is necessary to return to the next crucial phase in Peter Blake's development as a ruralist: the foundation in 1975 of the Brotherhood of Ruralists. To some extent he, Jann and Graham Ovenden working closely together had already formed, in all but name, a kind of brotherhood in the early 1970s. There is the feeling also, though, that the direction his art had taken since going to live in the country had led to a clear and growing divergence of attitude and a strong sense of artistic isolation from his close 60s friends. While choosing an exhibition in Bath during 1974, a renewed acquaintance with David Inshaw's work struck immediate and profound chords of sympathy and, in the conversations that followed first with David, and later with Graham and Ann Arnold, friends and neighbours of David's in Devizes, it became clear that here was a whole new group of painters (also including Annie Ovenden, Graham's wife) working in ways remarkably sympathetic to his own, exploring similar veins of imagery. It was out of the sense of euphoria and elation they all felt at finding each other that the Brotherhood was founded, and the conviction that the strength and unity they all gained by these common bonds of sympathy and friendship required some firm public declaration of association. That story has already been told in the catalogue accompanying the touring exhibition *The Brotherhood of Ruralists* in 1981. Worth emphasising again however is that there was never, as the Definitive Nudes make clear, a question of forming a common style, though the current of feeling that runs between them is still very apparent.

In artistic terms, the Brotherhood had a considerable influence on Peter Blake's work. 'Titania', referred to earlier, is the outstanding example, encouraging him to apply on a much grander and more elaborate scale the meticulous style first hinted at in 'Puck'. It is an astonishing work, marking the high point of his fascination with the imaginative world that his own children had allowed him to enter, capturing something of their gift to move at will and in a flash between their fantasy world, believing in both at the same time and with equal vehemence.

While trying to put himself imaginatively in the child's place, he is also well aware that he cannot escape the fact of his own adulthood and sexuality and it is this mixture of eroticism and innocence which make 'Titania' such a powerful contemporary image. Crucial to its impact is the way it 'tells a story' and of course the hallucinatory effect of the incredibly precise technique, worthy at times of the very best Victorian art. She is the only truly successful twentieth-century attempt at a fairy painting, still sufficiently disturbing to upset and arouse considerable antagonism yet without a trace of whimsy.

'Titania' has been worked on over a considerable period; there is and perhaps could not be another work quite like it. The other fairy portraits, a vivid, enchanting but also rather disturbing gallery of mischievous children, are all on a much smaller scale, while the only other large work of recent years, 'Ophelia' (1978–79), part of an earlier Ruralist project, is very different in mood and technique. Sombre and dark, comparatively sketchily painted apart from the hypnotic eyes, it is an image of suffering and anguish that reflects the crisis in his own family life at this time.

Back and settled in London, the Ruralist movement for him may be over. A new pattern has yet to be fully established. It may be unwise to place the Ruralist idea entirely in the past however – the sculpture parks derive from beach-combing on the shores of North Cornwall during the annual Ruralist holiday – and the habits and attitudes formed in the course of ten years may well be seen to have left their permanent and continuing mark on his achievement.

Nicholas Usherwood

THE DURABLE EXPENDABLES OF PETER BLAKE

Peter Blake has a mania for the plastic give-away that rivals Kurt Schwitters' appetite for rubbish. But apart from the fact that their productions are directed towards the Fine Art consumer, they have little else in common. Schwitters was a salvationist. When he picked a dirty old tram ticket out of the gutter it was with the intention of modifying its identity by absorbing it into an artistic composition. Like all salvationists, he was drunk with the power of his own personality. He saw the tram ticket as a tram ticket only for polemical reasons; only to proclaim that genius does not need costly materials in order to create great works of art. He recognised it primarily as a piece of nameless colour and texture to be worked with other oddments into an artistic whole. He saved it in order to consume it. In this sense he subscribed, like most twentieth-century artists, to the Cézannian aesthetic. Sir Herbert Read introduced his 'Critics Choice' exhibition with these words: 'Cézanne's aim, rigorously followed, has led step by step with inexorable logic to the kind of painting I have chosen for this exhibition.' I think he was right, but what we saw was a series of impoverishments leading with inexorable logic to a smooth one-colour sheet of paint. When Cézanne began to eliminate descriptive values from his work as being merely contingent to pictorial values he took the first step which brought about

the great twentieth-century experiment in expendability. One by one the pictorial values have gone the same way as the descriptive values (someone once said of Nicholson's white reliefs that 'they go further still than the pictures of Mondrian, which never gave up the relations of colour') and it must afford Rayner Banham a good deal of pleasure to observe that the 'Fine Art Boys' have treated 'Cézanne's aim' as if it were no different from comics and plastic give-aways.

One implication of the stepping-up of the expendability rate of formal concepts in the twentieth century is that the Fine Arts have all along been part and parcel of pop culture, and the odd thing is that Peter Blake, who attended many meetings of the Independent Group of the ICA and must have heard many hymns in praise of expendability, is trying to preserve comics and plastic give-aways from the fate meted out to 'Cézanne's aim'. His art proposes what Reyner Banham would call a flat contradiction in terms: it is dedicated to the Durable Expendable.

Rewald, in his *History of Impressionism*, records that Berthe Morisot was amazed and hurt when she heard Degas explain to Mallarmé that 'an artist is only an artist at certain hours . . . objects possess the same appearance for everyone', but most pop-art painters would agree with both halves of Degas' contention. One can take Larry

Rivers' painting of rows of variations on a Camel cigarette pack as an example. Not one of them is a straight copy and everyone is different. It is a demonstration of the transforming power of the artist during working hours, dependent upon the idea that a Camel pack possesses the same appearance for everyone. This kind of picture is usually supposed to disclose the artist's affectionately ironical attitude towards his subject-matter. Actually, it is a deliberately contemptuous approach, intended to spotlight the *belle peinture*; a kind of built-in art-appreciation gimmick.

I think Peter Blake would endorse only the second half of Degas' contention. ('Objects possess the same appearance for everyone.') He is too interested in the nature of a thing as he finds it to wish to modify its identity. He wants to display all the processed and pre-packed objects which are the substance of his art with a minimum of distortion. He is well aware of the transforming power of selection and juxtaposition, but tries to counter their effect by according the objects high visibility and presenting them without rhetoric. His work is a declaration of his interests, intransigent to the point of naïvety.

It leads him into some curious experiments in identification. A strip called 'Only Sixteen' which he contributed to *Ark* is conceived in the spirit of the genre and is not a joke against it. It opens with the boy saying to the girl 'Are you my blind date? Why you're only a blooming school-kid!' and ends with the boy and the girl in a heart-shaped frame and the boy saying: 'You're the teen-queen for me – always.' Even the interjection 'In *Ark's* tender breathtaking love stories all your dreams come true' does not operate as a send-up. The cliché content is preserved throughout. Another strip contributed to a subsequent issue of *Ark* is

more fragmentary but in a way more ambitious, and in the first frame the integration of lettering and images to convey information on a subliterate level is a first-class professional job of its peculiar kind. The 'chortling' villain has blown up a house and with a tongue rising behind his bottom set like the bust of a starlet he shouts into a bubble: 'Ha! Ha! That's my bad turn done for the day.' Explosive words mingle with the debris: 'Bang! Blam!! Pop, Crunch!' I may be wrong, but the use of the word 'pop' (without an exclamation mark) looks to me like a gleam of humour, as if Blake were pretending that he had heard someone burst a paper bag just as the house blew up. Otherwise, the work done on this frame seems to constitute a serious attempt to reach the l.a.c. of the strips. The fact that it was reproduced in a student's *avant garde* magazine turns it into a laughing matter, but the effect of semi-moronic energy achieved in the draughtsmanship appears to me to be the result of a not at all funny experiment in self-abasement.

When he was still a student at the Royal College of Art Blake became interested in the work of some of the American symbolic-realists: Ben Shahn, Bernard Perlin (whose 'Orthodox Boys' is in the Tate) and in particular Honoré Sharrer. He was more interested in their realism (and the American folk tradition in which it is rooted) than their symbolism, which contrives a liberalist prepackaging of their observations of the American scene, and although the influence of Sharrer can be observed in some of his early paintings they bear no trace of the schoolmarmish attitude which in practice starches her declared intention to 'praise and caress the great majority'. Blake does not see himself as an advocate of the great majority but as a member of it: he is the schoolboy who collects badges and the teenager who puts Elvis

Presley again and again at the top of the hit parade: he has the faculty of growing up without shedding his childhood and adolescence.

It was at *The Observer* Exhibition of Portraits of Children held in 1955 that I first saw a painting by Peter Blake. It depicted two blankly staring little boys with badges pinned all over their lapels as if they were members of twenty or thirty different clubs, leagues and associations, and in his 'Self Portrait with Badges', painted in 1961, he openly declares his solidarity with them: so much so, indeed, that it might well be a portrait of one of the boys as an adult who, with the passing of the years, has, not unnaturally, acquired more insignia. It is one of the most endearing and certainly one of the most truthful self-portraits painted in our time; and no painter could be more deserving of 'decorations and orders', for, in the course of the six years that separate these two paintings, Blake has turned the schoolboy cult of badge-collecting into an enveloping image of society.

The oil of the two schoolboys was probably painted before he saw any of Sharrer's work, but the painting which he calls 'The Balcony', completed two or three years later, took its point of departure from Sharrer's 'Workers and Pictures', which was included in the cross-section of the Museum of Modern Art's twentieth-century American collection exhibited at the Tate in 1956. Sharrer's picture depicts a row of working-class family groups against a background of tenements and factories, and every family is standing behind a famous painting as if it were its only possession or even as if it were the work of one of its members. It would seem to be an illustration of Simone Weil's dictum that 'second-class works or below are suitable for the élite and absolutely first-class works for the people', but although it is skil-fully done it strikes a false and patronising note. Blake's picture is thematically and pictorially a much more sophisticated work. It is called 'The Balcony' because it contains a reproduction of a famous balcony painting by Monet and photographs of the Royal Family on the balcony at Buckingham Palace, but it is also a metaphor for the act of 'coming out into the open', of acknowledging what one stands for. It depicts four young people sitting on a bench and another standing on a table behind them but cut off at the waist by the top edge of the canvas. One's first impression is that their teacher has been enquiring into their private lives and has asked them to pose for a photograph whilst in the act of displaying the sort of thing they pin up on their bedroom walls, but a closer look at the mixture of magazine covers, newspaper photographs, badges and printed packages reveals little samples of 'high paste' and action painting and a reference to the death of John Minton and to Bratbys' kitchen table still-lifes which indicate that the children are, so to speak, acting on his behalf. They are displaying a cross-section of his own visual environment in which the specialist interests of an art student mingle with interests which he still actively shares with them. This somewhat ambiguous device has its formal counterpart in the flattened spatial effect which suggests both a patch of grass and a green baize notice board and in the use of paint to simulate collage.

It marked an important stage in his development and is probably his most complex achievement to date, but there is a sense in which its sophistication and subtleties overplay themselves. At all events, he seems in all his later work to be aiming at simpler design and more forthright impact. At the same time, he is very sparing in his use of material that has associations only for a minority. But in this last connection and especially when he is paying homage to some personage in show business, there is sometimes a double standard at work. His choice falls on 'pop' rather than 'minority pop' figures, but some of them seem to be chosen partly for the delectation of his 'far-out' friends, as if they were the object of a special cult. One has the impression that he and his circle enjoy a peculiar sense of superiority when they come across anyone who does not know that the word 'Tuesday' for instance, spelt out large in one of his paintings, refers to the film actress Tuesday Weld. Probably any young person off the street could instantly match the word with the photograph in the same picture, but the impression remains that the image is being used as what I will call an IG(ICA)RCA goody, in the hope that the term carries for the reader an implication of inverted culture-snobbery, and it seems to confirm Reyner Banham's contention in the article on another page to which I have constantly referred, that 'Peter Blake's Pop art paintings are a mass of goodies'. Yet Blake himself appears to think that even when using what he takes to be a goody, some knowledge of the person whose photograph is the subject-matter of his picture is necessary to the communication. This is made clear by his embarrassingly helpful little note about two pictures of Sammy Davis Jr. in the catalogue of his first Portal Gallery exhibition. 'I would like to explain,' he wrote, 'for anyone who might not know, that Sammy Davis Jr. is an American entertainer, hip, one-eyed "Jewish-Negro".'

Fortunately, one's appreciation of his pictures are not dependent on an awareness of a goody-content or one's ability to identify a particular person. It so happens that small circular cut-outs of both Tuesday Weld and Sammy Davis Jr. appear in the collage of his which pretends to be a case of medals. I did not recognize them until long after I had grown especially fond of this work, and the additional information made no difference to the pleasure it afforded me. I had already accepted them, in a context of badges, trade labels, old coins and other odds-and-ends, as contemporary faces suitable for good conduct medals – a laughing girlie face and a grimacing negro singer face. The collage makes an exquisite off-beat decoration and reads like the accent of an average life of passing enthusiasms, erotic daydreams and inadequate hobbies.

In the first appreciation of Peter Blake's work to appear in print, Roger Coleman feared that Blake might be tempted to use his ready-made material for its own sake and not for what he could make of it formally. My own contention is that he does indeed use ready-made images for their own sake, but that the meaningfulness of his work arises – like the work in almost any art tradition – from the interdependence of the subject-matter and its presentation. In the collage-paintings which now constitute the greater part of his output, the subject-matter is an image or a collection of images already processed by mechanical reproduction, and this subject-matter remains sacrosanct in that it is never deliberately altered or 'interpreted', and since there is never any overlapping of images or any other kind of artistic placing, the pictorial presentation is confined to the relationship between the images and their support. The support is basically, and logically enough, a board for displaying notices. This board is sometimes treated as a plain, uninterrupted surface or is divided into compartments by beading, and sometimes as a door or part of a door: it is painted in clean, bright solid colours which bring to mind the colours used for the traditional decoration of fairground booths, caravans and barges. This connection with the popular art of another time has a way of thrusting Elvis Presley, Kim Novak and all the pin-up starlets into a kind of imaginary Edwardian period where they acquire before their time something of the charm, the quaintness and the pathos of performers and entertainers gone for ever.

The collage-paintings with their hard enamelled colour and the paintings with their soft, matt, powdery tonalities seem to many people to be so sharply distinct from one another as to suggest divided allegiances, but both aspects of his art disclose an affinity with the artist-craftsmen who used to work directly for the common people. His art is static and contemplative. He is faithful to his ready-made material but he has the power to look at a hand-tinted postcard of Edwardian lovers in a circle of forget-me-nots, or a pin-up photograph that has been whistled at by a million youths or a likeness of Elvis that has watched an army of virgins undress as if this were all of beauty that he had ever known or ever needed to know. He finds human warmth where others find only clichés and exploitation.

Robert Melville
Reprinted from *Motif* 10, Winter 1962/3

LIST OF PLATES

These appear in chronological order

Self Portrait (In RAF Jacket) c.1952–3
Cat.no.140, p.41

Children reading Comics 1954
Cat.no.4, p.42

On the Balcony 1955–7
Cat.no.15, p.43

Siriol, She-Devil of Naked Madness 1957
Cat.no.22, p.44

Couples 1959
Cat.no.72, p.45

Girlie Door 1959
Cat.no.31, p.46

Got a Girl 1960–1
Cat.no.47, p.47

Self Portrait with Badges 1961
Cat.no.19, p.48

Toy Shop 1962
Cat.no.37, p.49

Big Do-Nut Drive In 1963
Cat.no.223, p.50

The Beatles 1963–8
Cat.no.51, p.51

Jean Harlow 1964
Cat.no.224, p.52

Le Petit Porteur 1964–5
Cat.no.76, p.53

**Portrait of David Hockney in a
Hollywood–Spanish Interior** begun 1965
Cat.no.102, p.54

Kamikaze 1965
Cat.no.56, p.55

Monarch of the Glen 1965–8
Cat.no.82, p.56

Roxy Roxy 1965–83
Cat.no.62, p.57

Babe Rainbow 1967
Cat.no.63, p.58

Girl in a Poppy Field 1968–9
Cat.no.148, p.59

'"But it isn't old!" Tweedledum cried'
1970–1
Cat.no.156, p.60

'"Well this is grand!" said Alice' 1970–1
Cat.no.160, p.61

Liberty Blake in a Kimono 1971
Cat.no.161, p.62

Flowers in a Vase or A Posy for Liberty 1972
Cat.no.163, p.63

The Tuareg 1972
Cat.no.164, p.64

Titania 1972–4
Cat.no.84, p.65

Souvenir for Kitaj 1974
Cat.no.120, p.66

A Little Museum for Tom Phillips 1977
Cat.no.123, p.67

Titania 1976–83
Cat.no.85, p.68

Daimler 1980
Cat.no.233, p.69

Portrait of Richard Guyatt 1981
Cat.no.80, p.70

Poppy Fairy 1981–2
Cat.no.95, p.71

The Owl and the Pussycat 1981–3
Cat.no.97, p.72

Self Portrait (In RAF Jacket) c.1952–3

Children reading Comics 1954

On the Balcony 1955–7

Siriol, She-Devil of Naked Madness   1957

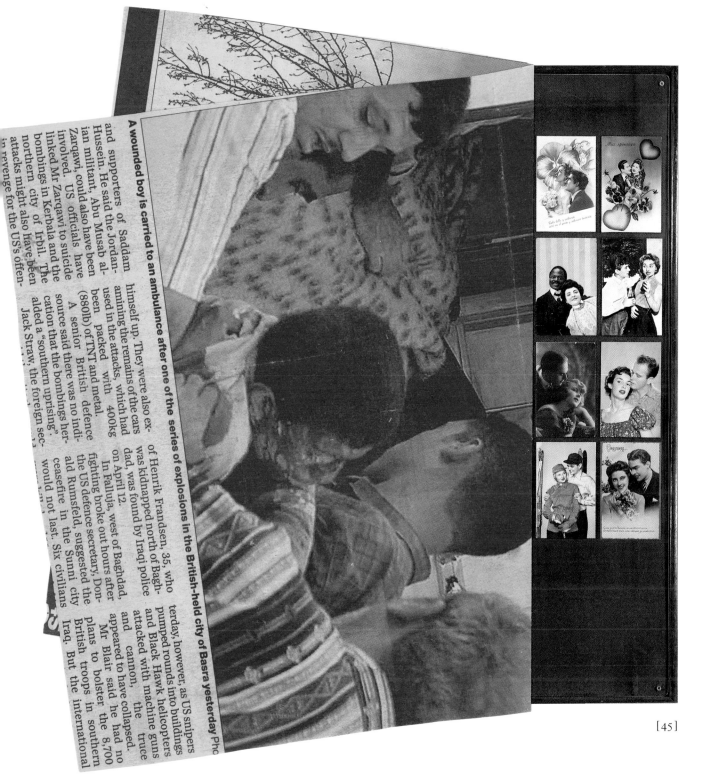

A wounded boy is carried to an ambulance after one of the series of explosions in the British-held city of Basra yesterday Pho

and supporters of Saddam Hussein. He said the Jordanian militant, Abu Musab al-Zarqawi, could also have been involved. US officials have linked Mr Zarqawi to suicide bombings in Kerbala and the northern city of Irbil. The attacks might also have been in revenge for the US's offen-

himself up. They were also examining the remains of the cars used in the attacks, which had been packed with 400kg (880lb) of TNT and metal.

A senior British defence source said there was no indication that the bombings heralded a "southern uprising".

Jack Straw, the foreign sec-

of Henrik Frandsen, 35, who was kidnapped north of Baghdad, was found by Iraqi police on April 12.

In Falluja, west of Baghdad, fighting broke out hours after the US defence secretary, Donald Rumsfeld, suggested the ceasefire in the Sunni city would not last. Six civilians

terday, however, as US snipers pumped rounds into buildings and Black Hawk helicopters attacked with machine guns and cannon, the truce appeared to have collapsed.

Mr Blair said he had no plans to bolster the 8,700 British troops in southern Iraq. But the international

Girlie Door 1959

Got a Girl   1960–1

Self Portrait with Badges 1961

Peter Blake Los Angeles Nov 1963   **Big Do–Nut Drive In**   1963

The Beatles 1963–8

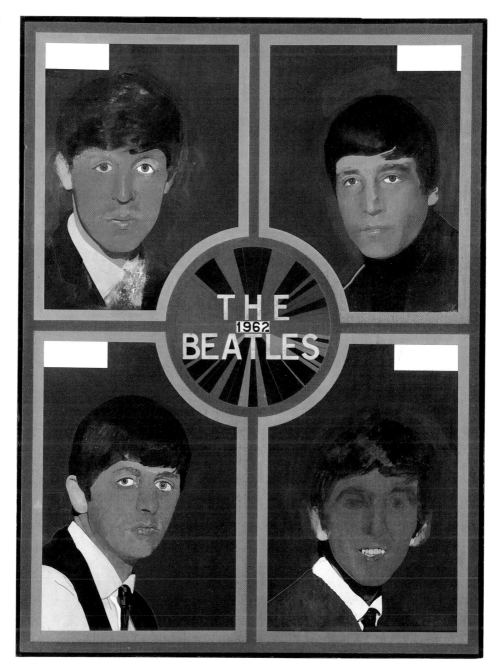

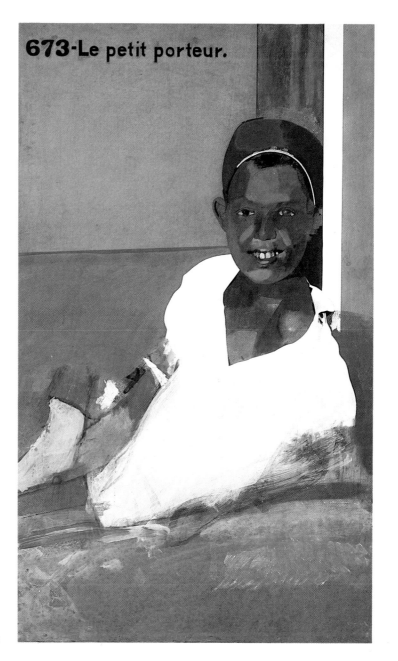

Le Petit Porteur   1964–5

**Portrait of David Hockney in
Hollywood-Spanish Interior**
begun 1965

Kamikaze 1965

AFTER 'THE MONARCH OF THE GLEN' BY SIR EDWIN LANDSEER. PETER BLAKE. 1966.

Left
Monarch of the Glen   1965–8

Right
Roxy Roxy   1965–83

Babe Rainbow 1967

Girl in a Poppy Field   1968–9

'"But it isn't old!" Tweedledum cried'
1970–1

'"Well this is grand!" said Alice'
1970–1

Liberty Blake in a Kimono
1971

**Flowers in a Vase or
A Posy for Liberty** 1972

THE TUAREG

Titania   1972–4

Souvenir for Kitaj   1974

A Little Museum for Tom Phillips 1977

Titania 1976–83

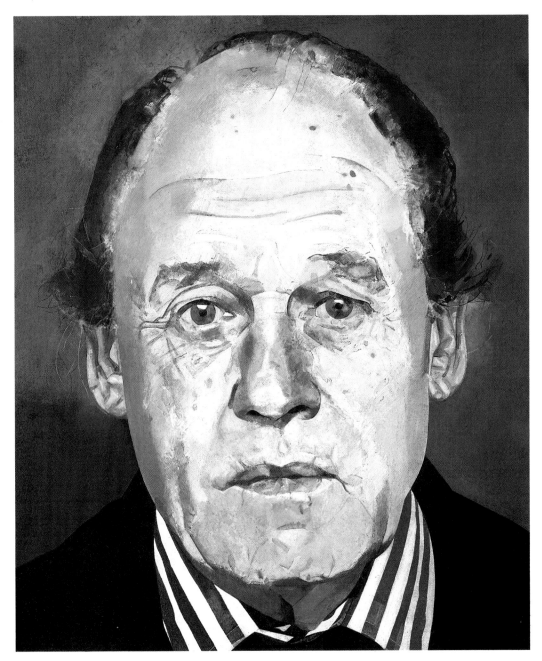

Left
Portrait of Richard Guyatt
1981

Right
Poppy Fairy 1981-2

The Owl and the Pussycat 1981–3

CATALOGUE

In the catalogue entries dimensions are given in inches followed by centimetres in brackets; height precedes width.

Some of the information which follows is drawn from the catalogues of the exhibitions at the Robert Fraser Gallery (Robert Melville) 1965, Bristol City Art Gallery (Francis Greenacre) 1969, Kunstverein Hamburg (Uwe Schneede) and Waddington Galleries 1977, all based for the most part on interviews with the artist. The rest is directly based on the same. Inverted commas are used to indicate either personal assumed roles or vocabulary of the artist or, where the context indicates more public formulae.

BOYS AND GIRLS
THE YOUNG ARTIST'S
WORLD

1   Self Portrait 1949
Oil on hardboard
$11\frac{3}{4} \times 9 (29.9 \times 22.8)$
Waddington Galleries

Probably the first oil painting by Blake, painted while at Gravesend School of Art. This picture already establishes what were to be some of the recurrent features in his figure paintings: the frontal pose, the pronounced creases in the lower lip, the discontinuous surface and the fact that one eye is realised less completely than the other.

2   Portrait of Shirley Blake 1950
Oil on cardboard
$18 \times 12\frac{1}{4} (45.7 \times 31.1)$
Shirley Norfolk

The artist's sister, aged about 16, painted in a style that derives ultimately from Flemish portraits in the National Gallery.

3   The Deluge 1953–4
Oil on board
$13\frac{3}{4} \times 18 (35 \times 45.7)$
Gordon and Jo House

Subject from the Old Testament, imagined as a contemporary girl.

4   Children reading Comics 1954
Oil on hardboard
$14\frac{1}{2} \times 18\frac{1}{2} (36.9 \times 47)$
Carlisle Museum and Art Gallery

Based on family snapshots of the artist and his sister when children.

Blake contributed two fictional pages of comics to *Ark*, the magazine of the Royal College.

The page from *Eagle* shown by the boy advertises 'boy's' things: Meccano and free gifts. The girl's page, from the same comic, seems to be a romance: 'You are wounded Prince!'

5   Boy and Pigeons *c.*1954
Oil on hardboard
$19 \times 10\frac{1}{4} (48.3 \times 26)$
Mrs Stoutzker

Painted from a family photograph of Blake's brother or cousin in Trafalgar Square, where being photographed feeding pigeons is a long established popular ritual.

6 Litter 1955
Oil on board
$13\frac{1}{2} \times 9\frac{1}{2}(34.3 \times 24)$
Sheffield City Art Galleries

A *trompe l'oeuil* still-life of the kind traditionally composed as a wall mounted board but Blake presents it as rubbish lying on the ground plane. The objects in the picture are of the same kind as he was to collect on his travels and even include a card of a bull-fight which resembles the pack of Cuba Blend at the top of 'On the Balcony'. In the 50s a slightly new significance was given to the 'urban detritus' which had earlier been collected and used by Schwitters and others. It was interpreted in terms of 'information' or of anthropological data. Blake offers it without implied comment. The boots worn by the figure who disappears at the top are the base-ball boots fashionable in the art world at the time and could be those of Blake looking down at the world he lives in.

7a Boys with New Ties *c.*1955
Oil on hardboard
$12\frac{1}{4} \times 29\frac{1}{2}(31.1 \times 74.9)$
Mrs Jinty Stephenson

This picture uses a device to which Blake resorted much later in 'Rosseweisse' (Cat. no. 87) of 'cutting off' the top of the head so as to emphasise the importance of the main feature, here the ties. It is a device which may be seen in advertising.

7b ABC Minors 1955
Oil on hardboard
$28\frac{3}{4} \times 18\frac{1}{4}(73 \times 46.3)$
Saarland Museum Saarbrücken

'ABC Minors' refers to a Saturday morning cinema club for children. Peter Blake was a member during the war and kept his badge.

8 Adam and Eve *c.*1954–5
Oil on hardboard
$18 \times 10\frac{1}{2}(45.7 \times 26.7)$
Private collection

Both are dressed in contemporary garments, Eve in a jewelled G-string like that Blake was to devise for circus artistes.

Painted at the Royal College in the academic year 1954–5. Almost the whole of the output of the previous year, his first at the College, was left in his locker and disappeared. About six small self portraits and some life paintings were lost.

8

are holding the props for a Sunday-school play. The picture contains a representation of a sculpture in the Victoria & Albert Museum of Christ on a donkey and a well-known engraving of Jerusalem. The donkey is a Mobo Bronco. The ground plane is painted in the vertical dimension so that the curb and pavement of the street in which the group are standing appears at the top.

The device that he was to use later, of a picture being used as a mask, appears here in the form of the engraving which is held up on a small pole like a banner.

10   Children reading Comics 1956
Oil on hardboard
$15\frac{1}{2} \times 11\frac{1}{2}(39.4 \times 29.2)$
Royal College of Art

9   The Preparation for the Entry into Jerusalem 1955–6
Oil on hardboard
$50 \times 40(127 \times 101.6)$
Royal College of Art

'The Entry into Jerusalem' was the set subject for the Rome Scholarship at the Royal College in 1955. Blake has changed it to the 'Preparation for . . .' so as to bring in figures of children who

Related to Children reading Comics (Cat. no. 4)

The figures have been brought up close so that the comics occupy the picture plane which they divide into a sort of grid. Blake developed this scheme in works like 'Girls with their Hero' and 'Sammy Davis Jr' (Cat. nos 42 and 43)

12

11 Portrait of Joe in Spain 1957
Oil on board
$8\frac{1}{2} \times 8(21.6 \times 20.3)$
Private collection

Painted from life. The sitter is Joe Tilson who was a student at the Royal College with Blake. A photograph exists showing both Blake and Tilson, who wears the same Basque beret, in a similar landscape.

12 Guardia Civil 1957
Oil on hardboard
$11\frac{1}{4} \times 8\frac{1}{4}(28.5 \times 21)$
Erik and Lilott Berganus

Painted from life. The sitter was the local policeman in the village near Tarragona where Blake stayed with Joe Tilson, during his travels on his Leverhulme scholarship to study popular arts. The policeman would pause each day for half an hour while Blake painted.

13 Goldfish 1957
Oil on hardboard
$9 \times 7\frac{1}{4}(22.9 \times 18.4)$
Waddington Galleries

Painted from the round goldfish pond at the British School in Rome. A floating leaf and matchstick, which appear to lie on the surface of the picture, are a characteristic reference to the 'problem' of the picture plane in twentieth century art.

14 Shoe on the Beach at Nice 1957
Oil on hardboard
$7\frac{1}{4} \times 6(18.4 \times 15.2)$
Mrs Stoutzker

Painted on the same visit as no. 191.

13

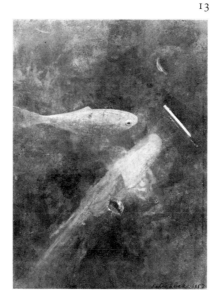

15 On the Balcony 1955–7
Oil on canvas
$47\frac{3}{4} \times 35\frac{3}{4}(121.3 \times 90.8)$
Tate Gallery

The subject was set for the Royal College of Art Diploma in 1955 but the picture was not completed until Blake returned to England in 1957. As in Cat. nos 8 and 9, Blake has brought a traditional subject into his world of Boys and Girls. The prototype for his treatment was a painting by the social realist Honoré Sharrer in the Museum of Modern Art, New York. This painting, 'Workers and their Pictures', showed contemporary workers holding masterpieces of modern art that they could never possess as individuals. It came to London for the 1955 exhibition of American Art at the Tate but was not hung. Blake made an appointment to see it in storage at the American Embassy.

Two of Blake's boys hold paintings and they are surrounded by all sorts of references to the theme of which the most definitive is the painting by Manet represented as a framed reproduction left. The rest of the twenty-seven or so include newspaper and magazine clippings, illustrations and drawings.

This theme in the painting is interwoven with the set subject in a topical way. The four pictures represented are by Dick Smith (centre in a frame), below it a Robyn Denny from which paint seems to trickle on to the edge of the park bench, at the bottom a Leon Kossoff in an appropriate frame invented by Blake. All three were fellow students of Blake. The picture held by the boy on the right is by Blake's brother. The painting leaning up against this is a 'litter' picture by Blake himself, on which is pinned a drawing which has been left incomplete and then used as a palette for testing colours. The still life on the table, left, is an allusion to the 'Kitchen Sink' paintings of the previous generation at the College (John Bratby, Jack Smith etc.); on it is a copy of the *New Statesman* in which John Berger wrote in support of Social Realism. There is a little note apparently from Blake to himself ('What Balcony'). The table at the top is both a stage prop for a school performance of the balcony scene in Romeo and Juliet and Blake's own painting table. On it is a drawing, scribbled over for an 'On the Balcony', a two figure composition like the comics pictures. There are drawings by Matisse and apparently Steinberg. The death of the painter John Minton, who taught at the Royal College, is lamented in the photograph on the jersey of the boy on the right.

The children also have devices expressing their fictional interests and life style: badges, dark glasses and clothes including a tie on which is painted a girl who looks like the famous image of Marilyn Monroe holding her skirts down (Seven Year Itch). The boy wearing this tie is also wearing a paper hat and a cover of *Life Magazine* (British deb Julia Williamson September 1957) as a kind of mask.

Other themes are the picture-plane and the Royal family.

16   Boy with Paintings 1957–9
Oil and enamels on wood
12 × 10(30.5 × 25.4)
Private collection

A self portrait. The painting held by the boy in the left background (also a self portrait) was a Valentine for Pauline Boty, a rather later student at the Royal College, who was to die young. The tear in the eye of the main figure is however a conventional lament that she preferred someone else. The Valentine image appeared later in 'Love Wall' (Cat. no. 36) and in the design for 'Motif' 1962. The striped area to the right is a quotation of the pedestrian crossing pictures painted by Brian Young, another contemporary. However, this sort of heraldic device was to take a more integrated role in Blake's later 'Pop' pictures such as 'Tuesday' (Cat. no. 34).

16

17

P BLAKE

17 Still Life of Apples 1958
Oil on panel
$8\frac{1}{4} \times 6(21 \times 15.2)$
Fleur Cowles

One of several small still-lifes painted by Blake; another represents rounded pebbles. Both subjects appear in 'On the Balcony' (Cat. no. 15)

18 Cigarette Packet 1959–60
Oil on hardboard
$7 \times 5\frac{3}{4}(18 \times 14.5)$
Wolverhampton Art Gallery

Related to the rubbish paintings (Cat. no. 6). A similar picture is represented at the lower right of 'On the Balcony'.

20

19 Self Portrait with Badges 1961
Oil on hardboard
$68 \times 47\frac{1}{2}(172.7 \times 120.6)$
Tate Gallery

This picture is fully catalogued in the *Tate Gallery Illustrated Catalogue of Acquisitions 1978–80*. It was painted between June and September 1961 mainly from life (using a mirror) except the jacket, which was placed on a dummy. Although the clothes are those that Blake wore at the time and were bought with some effort, being very much ahead of the fashion, he did not in life cover himself with badges. Some had remained in his possession from childhood but he collected a great number. This element of the picture is a kind of museum.

The picture remained incomplete up to the time it was sent to the John Moore's Liverpool exhibition and won the junior prize. The landscape is very sketchy and, for example, only Blake's right boot is fully realised. The other is left to be conjectured from this and from the sample near the big toe which gives an account of the layers of rubber etc. at this point.

20 Boy with Hot Dog 1960–5
Cryla on hardboard
$14 \times 16(35.6 \times 40.6)$
Arts Council of Great Britain

This may be considered the last of the early realist series of pictures of boys and girls. The boy was depicted as sucking an ice-lolly when Blake started the picture in the summer of 1960 but he thought this inappropriate when he took it up again in the autumn and so changed it to a hot dog.

[79]

21

22

25

THE CIRCUS

**21　Loelia, World's Most Tattooed
Lady** 1955
Oil and collage on panel
$29\frac{1}{2} \times 10\frac{1}{2}(74.9 \times 26.7)$
Fleur Cowles

One of the series of circus ladies including also 'Siriol' (Cat. no. 22, painted on
another part of the same panel) and
'Dixie' (Cat. no. 24). These two pictures
resemble a painting by Otto Dix
'Zuleika the Tattooed Wonder', 1920.

The left eye, mouth and navel are
painted in a photographic style, the rest
in a fairground painter's style. The
tattoos appear to derive from comics,
posters and newspapers and seem to be
a reflection of the 'media environment'
and of Blake's own interests rather than
examples of the kinds of images generally produced by tattooists.

The figure has six arms like those of
the Hindu goddess of destruction, Kali.

**22　Siriol, She-Devil of Naked
Madness** 1957
Oil and collage on panel
$29\frac{1}{2} \times 8\frac{1}{2}(75 \times 21.6)$
Private collection

See Cat. no. 21. This picture was first
exhibited (ICA 1958) under the name
'Koochie Dancer' given it by someone
else! The picture is painted as a damaged object and Blake has carved his
initials on it. On the right there appears
to be a representation of a snow capped
volcano (Fujiyama?) that consorts with
the naval hat and suggests that Siriol is
a traveller.

**23　Cherie, Only Bearded
Tattooed Lady** 1957?
Oil on panel
$12 \times 7(30.5 \times 17.8)$
Private collection

**24　Dixie, Darling of the
Midway** 1955–8
Oil on panel
$12\frac{1}{2} \times 9\frac{1}{4}(31.7 \times 23.5)$
Richard Smith

Painted on a panel that had been used as
a palette. The paint that had dried and
wrinkled on it can be seen through
Blake's paint and was used by him to
give a rich 'old' surface.

25　Knife Thrower's Board 1957
Oil and collage on hardboard
$67\frac{1}{8} \times 19\frac{5}{8}(170.5 \times 49.9)$
Private collection

Based on the full-sized pin-up of
Brigitte Bardot published by *Reveille* on
several sheets. Most of the figure is
collage but the head is painted. The
flesh parts were covered with pink tis-
sue paper which has faded. The knives
(and forks) come from the cutlery
section of the catalogue for the Great
Exhibition of 1851.

26　Drum Majorette 1957
Oil and collage on hardboard
$36\frac{3}{8} \times 28\frac{1}{4}(92.4 \times 71.7)$
Private collection

The sunglasses are collaged on to the
panel as are the medals. The latter are a
miscellaneous collection of medal-
shaped objects including some sweets
which have disappeared. The ribbons
are painted. The idea derives partly
from Saul Steinberg.

27　Medals 1960
Collage on hardboard
$13\frac{1}{2} \times 10\frac{1}{2}(34.3 \times 26.7)$
Mr and Mrs Robert Melville

A belt near the lower edge implies that
this is the chest of a boy. The 'medals'
are a variety of mainly circular objects
stuck to the surface, with painted ribbons. The bonus in the work is a pris-
matic winking eye, lower right, new at
the time.

28　Gold Painting 1959
Gold leaf on canvas
$31 \times 21 \times \frac{3}{4}(78.7 \times 53.3 \times 1.9)$
Private collection

One of a number of gold paintings
exhibited at the New Vision Centre
1960.

Blake was exhibiting at about the
same time, pop music and film star
works at the ICA and object works like
the 'Toy Shop' at the Portal Gallery.
He thought it would be fun to exhibit a
third personality at the same time and
suggested this show to the owner with
Tony Gifford who exhibited sections of
football pitches. In the catalogue Blake
said his paintings represented sections
of Japanese screens but they also refer
to the monochromes of Yves Klein. The
gold pictures are further related to
collages made from cigarette-pack foil
and other materials made after his
Leverhulme award travels.

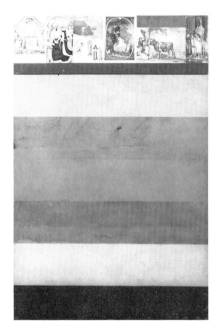

29   Fine Art Bit 1959
Enamel and collage on hardboard
36 × 24 × 1 (91.4 × 61 × 2.5)
Tate Gallery

Fully described in *Tate Gallery Biennial Report 1968–70*. The stripes in this picture refer both to the configuration of public art, including flags and street signs, and to contemporary abstract art which is contrasted with traditional 'Fine Art' in the form of postcards collected by Blake. The title, also, refers both to the bit of the picture in which the cards are set out and to the contemporary use of the word 'bit' to refer to an element of the culture ('the science fiction bit'). Blake had returned from the tour of Europe on which he was to study popular art but had also visited art museums. The picture within the Indian picture, centre, was a reference to his own similar practice.

A similar, but now destroyed, picture combined a row of pin-ups and a horizontally striped flag all collaged.

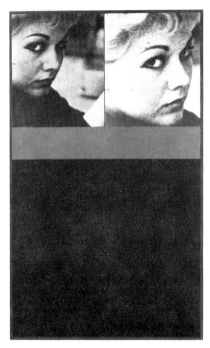

30   Kim Novak Wall 1959
Collage and enamel on hardboard
30 × 19 (76.2 × 48.3)
Mrs Garth Wood

The two pictures of the star are specially enlarged photographs taken from a publicity still. Blake was a particular fan of Novak and admired her as the innocent heroine of 'Bell, Book and Candle'. She appears also on the back of 'Locker' (Cat. no. 126). The rest of the panel is in shiny black lacquer intended to mirror the image of the person looking at it.

31   Girlie Door 1959
Collage and objects on hardboard
48 × 23¾ (121.9 × 59.1)
Private collection

The pictures in this collage come from Blake's collection of pin-ups. Several are of the 20s or earlier but most are of contemporary film stars including Gina Lollobrigida, Kim Novak, Elsa Martinelli, Shirley McLean and Marilyn Monroe in 'Some Like It Hot'. The door in this work, unlike the 'Love Wall' is painted in *trompe l'oeil*.

33 **The First Real Target** 1961
Collage on hardboard
20 × 18(50.8 × 45.7)
Tate Gallery

Comprising a Slazenger archery target and letters from an antique children's game. Blake bought a target from a sports shop in order to make this picture but lost it during the evening and had to buy a second! The reference is half-ironic, half in admiration of Jasper Johns.

Fully described in *Tate Gallery Illustrated Catalogue of Acquisitions 1974–76*. The subject, Tuesday Weld, was one of a group of teenage sex symbols of the late 50s and 60s. The pictures may have come from *Playboy*. She was chosen because people might not immediately associate the word 'Tuesday' with the image. For the use of stripes see 'The Fine Art Bit' above (Cat. no. 29). The first pop work in which they appeared was 'Elvis and Cliff' (not in exhibition). The use of letters in relief, wooden fillets etc. indicate that Blake thought of such works as objects like the locker (Cat. no. 126), windows and doors. It should also be said in the margin that some of the critical appraisal of abstract art in the twentieth century characterises painting as 'objects' rather than as 'representations'.

The letters of the name 'Tuesday' were bought from Woolworths but, since they had run out of A's, Blake inserted a V upside down as a 'deliberate mistake'.

32 **Valentine** *c.*1959–60
Enamels and collage on hardboard
24¾ × 18½(62.9 × 47)
Bryan Morrison

Made for Pauline Boty (see Cat. no. 16). The collage at the top includes material of the sort that he had collected in Europe and England.

33

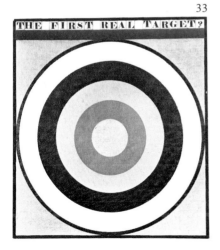

34 **Tuesday** 1961
Enamel paint, wood relief and collage on hardboard
18¾ × 10⅛ × 1½(47.6 × 25.7 × 3.9)
Tate Gallery

35 **Snap II** 1961
Oil and collage on hardboard
9⅞ × 14⅛(25.1 × 35.9)
Victoria and Albert Museum, London

Blake did two or three versions on this theme of which the largest has about twenty cards. The idea was to get the public to participate, to say 'Snap', at least silently in their heads.

36 **Love Wall** 1961
Collage construction
49½ × 81(125.7 × 205.7)
Fundação Calouste Gulbenkian Modern Art Centre, Lisbon

One of the most ambitious of Blake's collaged 'Pop works', it shares a format

36

with 'Toy Shop' (Cat.no.37) but
represents the more grown-up delights
of love. The images include a Millais
painting, numerous postcards and some
magazine pictures. The diagonal stripes
at the bottom are an allusion to
Westerman, the Chicago artist, whom
Blake admired. The number over the
door (twice) is 2, which could imply a
'couple'. The basis for this type of work
is the pin board on which Blake (like
many other people) collected images
that appealed to him.

The door is a real door, cut down.
The brackets of the porch were also
found, the rest constructed. The rec-
tangular section which now appears
white was formerly glass painted black
on the inside. This represented a

window, like that of a pub which had
been painted so as to be opaque and to
give back only the reflection of your face
instead of a glimpse of what was inside.
The fiction is that this is the front of a
shop where love may be found.

37 Toy Shop 1962
Collage construction
$60\frac{1}{2} \times 75\frac{1}{2}$ (153.7×191.7)
Tate Gallery

Fully described in the *Tate Biennial
Report 1968–70*.

This is both a work of art and a museum of toys collected by Blake. Its
forerunner was a trunk of toys, collected
by Blake's grandmother and kept for his

37

uncle until he returned from the war by which time he had grown out of them. Peter and his sister surreptitiously unpacked and played with them. Its successor is the Sculpture Park (Cat. no. 137) for which Blake began collecting in about 1970. Some of the toys relate ironically to art or to individual works like the 'Johns Targets'. The bonus in this work is the string of coloured lights. The door was a cupboard door and so appears child sized. The window was also found.

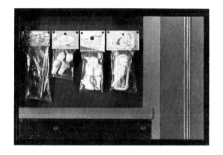

38   Five Dolls *c.*1962
Oil and collage on panel
$13\frac{1}{4} \times 20(33.7 \times 50.8)$
Waddington Galleries

This small work is a spin-off from 'Toy Shop'. Blake also thought of making a Christmas tree with gifts. There may be a slightly ironic reference here to the work of Arman and Spoerri, 'Nouveau Réalistes' who were shown at Gallery One.

**39   Girlie Door
(piece of a door)** 1962
Collage on panel
$19\frac{3}{8} \times 11\frac{1}{2}(48.9 \times 29.2)$
Waddington Galleries

Part of the same door as in Love Wall. The photographs are of European actresses, one of them being Monica Vitti.

39

40

40   Come Stanley! 1962
Matt black and white and black enamel paint on hardboard
$31\frac{3}{4} \times 36\frac{1}{4}(80.6 \times 92.1)$
Private collection

This picture represents a frame or caption from any one of a number of silent films in which Oliver Hardy uttered the catch phrase. It is the only work of its kind produced by Blake but it does refer to the kind of texts included in balloons in, for example, Lichtenstein's paintings of comics of which Blake had earlier produced his own painted versions. It precedes conceptual works comprising words only.

41   Girl in a Window 1962
Collage construction
$48\frac{3}{4} \times 44\frac{1}{2} \times 13\frac{3}{4}(123.8 \times 113 \times 34.9)$
Leeds City Art Galleries

Based on part of a real window. The feeling that this work is intended to evoke is the temptation and guilt associated with looking into other people's windows. A person who goes up to it to see what is partly hidden behind the curtains may be confronted with the wax head of a girl close to and suffer a slight shock of embarrassment.

ture. As in other early works, such as 'On the Balcony' (Cat.no.15) heroes are represented by their images in the mass media, fictionally collected by the real people in the painting. In later works the real person steps out of the picture but is imagined as the author or owner of it. However, here (as in other cases) the fans are drawn from the printed media, just as the stars are, apart from the girl, top right, who was painted from the same model as 'Pin Up' (Cat. no.69). Blake was already collecting Presley images before he started this picture and found others for it. He continued to collect afterwards but he stopped working on it, partly because Presley did not take the opportunity of his tour in the army in Europe to visit his numerous British fans.

Horizontal and vertical surfaces in the picture are both represented in the vertical picture plane so the space is hard to read. It is a working out of that in 'On the Balcony'. The images at the bottom are on boards leaning up against the legs of a table and there are further, framed pictures propped up against these. The next register, across the middle of the picture, is the table top. Above this, further images of Presley appear on a pin-board behind the fans. One of these is so large that it appears to be in life. The figure on the right seems to be in front of a door and, looking at the viewer is more 'real' than the fans. The space is therefore a series of flat, parallel planes.

42 Girls with their Hero 1959–62
Oil on hardboard
60 × 48(152.4 × 121.9)
Private collection

This was the first of Blake's pop music pictures. It shares with 'Sammy Davis Jr' (Cat.no.43) the idea of having the hero in quotation within a realist pic-

43 Portrait of Sammy Davis Jr
1960
Oil on hardboard
14½ × 12½(36.8 × 31.7)
Private collection

Peter Blake did two Sammy Davis Jr paintings, which were exhibited at the Portal Gallery in 1960. One was left as a 'Souvenir' for the entertainer at his

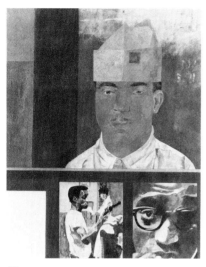

43

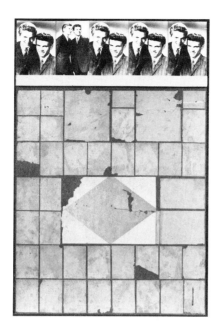

hotel and disappeared. This showed a girl holding a portrait of Davis and included at one time a portrait of Prince Rainier of Monte Carlo, later painted out. The man represented holding the pictures in the present version is wearing the kind of paper hat made by Italian carpenters and other workers. There is again a distant hint of Sharrer's 'Workers and their pictures' except that, of course, the pictures are photographs of the entertainer, not works of fine art.

44   Sinatra Door 1959
Collage and objects on hardboard
30 × 18(76.2 × 45.7)
Museum moderner Kunst Wien,
Österr. Ludwig Stiftung

The two identical photographs of Sinatra are publicity stills purchased from a record shop. The door element is 'trompe l'oeuil'. Blake was interested in the 'ratpack' reputation shared by Sinatra, Sammy Davis Jr and Dean Martin.

45   Everly Wall 1959
Collage on hardboard
36 × 24(91.4 × 61)
Terry Blake

The upper row comprises publicity stills of the Everly Brothers. Blake made another work using prints like the one second from the left. The repetition is a reference to Johns and Rauschenberg but more extreme. It precedes that of Warhol but alludes similarly to the mass production of pop imagery. The abstract part below comprises rectangles cut from newsprint and 'distressed' by Blake, with a paper flag found in Spain. It refers both to contemporary grid-based abstracts and to Schwitters to whose work Blake had been introduced by the painter Dick Smith. The flag also refers again to Johns.

46   El 1961
Lipstick and collage on wood
$11\frac{5}{8}$ × $8\frac{1}{4}$(29.5 × 21)
Private collection

One of several works employing images of the star. The picture of Elvis was found in a fan's scrapbook and bore the lipstick imprint of a kiss. This picture belongs to the group which have 'abstracts' painted below in such a way as to suggest that they are found objects.

47   Got a Girl 1960–1
Enamel, photo collage and record
37 × 61 × $1\frac{5}{8}$(94 × 154.9 × 4.2)
Whitworth Art Gallery,
University of Manchester

The pop stars are: Fabian, Frankie Avalon, Ricky Nelson, Bobby Rydell and two of Elvis Presley. The bonus in this work is the record of the same name by the Four Preps which expresses the frustration of a boy whose girl can only think of the pop stars, who appear in the picture, when ever he wants to kiss her.

47

lettering. The closing up of the crack through the 'R' in 'Vern' has produced a characteristic Blake contrived 'error'.

49   The Lettermen 1963
Oil on hardboard
49 × 73(124.5 × 185.4)
City of Kingston upon Hull
Museums and Art Galleries

Derived from a record sleeve. The Lettermen were a rock group who had or affected college origins and style like the Four Preps. The letters are the American equivalent of Oxbridge 'Blues'. The initial L, of course, stands for 'Lettermen'. This was a group whose music Blake admired and he also liked the image.

48

48   La Vern Baker 1961–2
Oil and collage on panel
$20\frac{1}{2} × 34\frac{1}{4}(52.1 × 87)$
Private collection

The head of the rock singer La Vern Baker is painted not collaged. The quarter sunburst motif is typical of fairground painting as is the style of the

50   Bo Diddley 1963
Cryla on hardboard
$48\frac{1}{4} × 30\frac{7}{8}(122.6 × 78.4)$
Museum Ludwig, Cologne

Based on a record sleeve. Blake has imitated and stressed the effects of cheap printing such as the red, yellow and blue-green fringes due to mis-registration. The fringes around the leg and guitar are in effect abstracted from this kind of error.

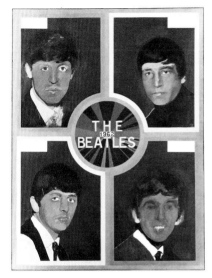

51   The Beatles 1963–8
Cryla on hardboard
48 × 36(121.9 × 91.4)
Private collection

Based on a page of a magazine showing
the group at the time of their return
from Germany in 1962. In 1963 they
suddenly became great stars. In the
meantime Blake had met them through
Robert Freeman.

The borders and 'fairground' central
panel are of a type that was fed back into
the typography of fan magazines, record
sleeves etc. by designers who had seen it
in pop art but, at the time the stills were
published, this had not yet happened
and they were plain. The blank panels
were intended for the Beatles to sign
but Blake eventually decided this was
not necessary.

The same effect of mis-registration
appears on the shoulders of the singers
here, as in Bo Diddley (Cat.no. 50) The
colours are the same as those of the
decorative margins.

53

54

52   Baron Adolf Kaiser 1961–3
Oil and enamel on hardboard
24 × 10(61 × 25.4)
Arts Council of Great Britain

The first of the wrestlers, it comprises only the fighter himself making a ritual threatening gesture and a 'cartoon' of him. The character is fictional but derived from an image in an American wrestling magazine. The shaven head is a typical mark of the 'teutonic villain', see also Doktor K. Tortur (Cat. no. 57). The wrestlers as a group descend from pictures of fairground strongmen in Blake's 'circus' style that were exhibited at the ICA 1958 but are now lost.

53   Irish Lord X 1963
Oil and collage on panel
20¾ × 14¾(52.7 × 37.5)
Private collection

A masked wrestler. The fiction within the fiction is that the wrestler has to wear a mask and call himself 'X' so that his family should not disown him.

The broken figure of an athlete on the frame had a mask painted to match that below. This 3D figure and a cut out portrait have since been lost.

54   Da Vinci Brothers 1963
Oil on panel
33 × 13⅜(83.8 × 34)
Private collection, Milan

A fictional tag team based on wrestling magazine pictures. They are imagined as having a false Italian identity. One of the figures at the top is mysteriously Chinese. The stencilled Christian names were added after the rest of the picture, the glass eye-patch originally a complete disc has been tucked under a fold of flesh so that it is held like a monocle.

55   Masked Zebra Kid 1965
Cryla and collage on panel
21¾ × 10½ × 1½(55.2 × 26.7 × 4)
Tate Gallery

Fully catalogued in *Tate Gallery Illustrated Catalogue of Acquisitions 1974–76*. This is probably the only real-life wrestler in the series. The pictures used as material for collage

55

56

57

came from a feature in *Boxing and Wrestling Illustrated*, an American publication. *Boxing* and *Wrestling* were later published separately and the latter was the main source of Blake's imagery. The signature in the centre is an autograph signed by the wrestler for the artist. The head has been deliberately darkened.

56 Kamikaze 1965
Cryla, collage on hardboard
31 × 18¾(78.7 × 47.6)
Private collection

An imaginary masked Japanese-American wrestler. Blake discovered later that there was an English wrestler using the same name which had been used to designate the pilots of light bombers trained to crash their planes suicidally on to allied ships in the Pacific Wars. A Japanese 'Zero' is on the left, a collaged picture of pilots right. Above is a traditional Japanese warrior's mask wearing in turn a fabric mask made by Jann Haworth to resemble that in the painting. The picture is reproduced without this detail in the Robert Fraser catalogue, 1965.

57 Doktor K. Tortur 1965
Cryla, collage on hardboard
24 × 10(61 × 25.4)
Erich Sommer

A second 'germanic' wrestler. This one is 'Doktor' (as in Doktor Caligari) and therefore doubly sinister. He is shown as affecting a certain degree of distinction: race horse, 1930s Mercedes, cigarette holder etc. The letters are from a nineteenth-century game. The missing parts of the figure of a wrestler at the top are intended to indicate that (as in the picture) the artist has not visualised the whole person but exhibits it incomplete like the Venus de Milo. It seems to be a very inappropriate figurine of a female goddess to which Blake has added a moustache and tights.

58 Kid McCoy 1965
Cryla, collage on wood
23 × 11⅛(58.4 × 29)
Private collection

The only boxer among the fighters and a real, historic person, distinguished for having invented the bolus punch. He was world welter-weight champion in 1896. This painting is left unfinished, for example, the right forearm and hand can hardly be discerned. The outline of the left shoulder is reimposed on a scumbled highlight, representing touching up in the boxing magazine photograph from which it was painted. There is an artificial hole in the panel which has been given the character of wear like that on a dartboard. The worm holes were made by hammering nails into the panel.

Blake wanted the picture to appear old since the boxer won his championship in 1896. His American nationality is declared in his stars and stripes sash. The little flag wrapped round the waist of the figure seems to have been added by an owner but is quite acceptable to the artist.

59 Little Lady Luck 1965
Cryla, collage on hardboard
28½ × 13¾(72.4 × 34.9)
Private collection

An imaginary lady wrestler, derived from a picture in a 'girlie' magazine, she is surrounded by lucky devices and charms as well as objects referring to horse-racing etc. where luck is so important. The rainbow colouring of the name hints at the legendary 'Pot of Gold at the End of the Rainbow'. She seems to be Irish. Outside the 'luck zone', on top of the frame are four china figures representing her at four ages, all in a tea-shop style quite different from the sophisticated style of the main figure. Since it was reproduced in the Robert Fraser 1965 catalogue it has been developed by adding the four objects in a row below the valentine and number 7 and the two outermost badges on the belt, the jacket has been extended, the hairstyle brought up-to-date and other alterations made.

59

60 Frisco and Lorenzo Wong and Wildman Michael Chow 1966
Cryla and collage over photograph
81 × 27(205.7 × 68.6)
Mr Chow

Based on a picture of a tag team (pair) in a wrestling magazine. Blake collaged on the heads, including that of Michael

Chow, the restaurant owner, as the manager. The whole group was enlarged photographically and then improved by painting. The team are imagined to be Chinese/Italian, a reference to Michael Chow's pioneering use of Italian waiters in a Chinese restaurant. The original name of the team was the Kangaroos and the manager was 'Wild Red Berry'.

61 Franck and Jesse, the James Brothers 1966–83
Cryla and collage on hardboard
18 × 16¼(45.7 × 41.3)
Private collection

A fictional tag-team of wrestlers styled as cowboys, and named after the almost mythical bank robbers. The name of one is spelt by a contrived 'error' in a teutonic way. The heads are painted after pictures of Sean Connery and

Steve McQueen. The figures on the top of the frame were painted by Chrissy Wilson. They represent the characters as heroes.

62 Roxy Roxy 1965–83
Cryla, enamel and collage on panel
26 × 20⅛(66 × 51.1)
Private collection

Conceived as an English wrestler who fights in America. The badges and other details identify her as British and, as work has continued on the picture, more and more improbably old-fashioned. The ship which appears both as a model and as a postcard is imagined to be that on which she travelled to America.

Her hairstyle has changed in 1982 having been bobbed formerly as in 'Les Orchidées Noires'.

63 Babe Rainbow 1967
Cryla and collage on hardboard
27½ × 18¾(69.8 × 47.6)
Private collection

Commissioned by Dodo Designs, originally to be an enamel plaque. When this proved impossible the design was silk-screened on to tin. 10,000 were printed and at one stage it sold for £1, making it one of the few genuine multiples available to anyone. It was developed from a 1967 cover of the French women's magazine *Marie Claire*. The features of the face are similar to those in the cover but have been modified by referring to other prototypes, the nose, for example, is 'broken'. Blake wrote an explanatory note for Dodo Designs:

'Babe Rainbow, a fictitious lady wrestler, is the most recent in a line of wrestlers I have painted. These include Irish Lord X, Doktur K. Tortur, Kamikaze and Les Orchidées Noires. She is twenty-three years old and has broken

her nose in the ring. She was born in New Cross, London and wrestles mainly in Europe and the U.S.A. as there have only been a few contests between lady wrestlers in London. She is the daughter of the notorious Doktur K. Tortur.'

64 La Petite Reine Africaine 1968–83
Cryla, enamel and collage on hardboard
24 × 13⅞(61 × 35.3)
Waddington Galleries

A wrestler who is imagined to be black and an African princess. The face derives from a magazine photograph of an American male black rights campaigner, the hairstyle is from an advertisement in a women's magazine of the 60s.

65 Blanche Neige and Bet Noir 1976–81
Oil on panel
$20\frac{1}{2} \times 13\frac{1}{4}(52.1 \times 33.7)$
Galerie Meyer-Ellinger, Frankfurt

A fictional ladies tag-team. The picture is illustrated in the Waddington Galleries catalogue 1977 in a much less complete state. The names are meant to carry overtones. Blanche Neige means Snow White but Blanche is also a christian name; Bet = Bête (Noire).

66 Nudina 1961–4
Oil on hardboard
$13\frac{3}{8} \times 6\frac{7}{8}(34 \times 17.5)$
Private collection, Stuttgart

An imaginary stripper who is a fan dancer. The diagonal form across the body is to suggest the feathers of a fan whirling by. The china figure at the top was chosen because Blake associated ostrich feathers with picture hats. The style of the figure suggests the effect of a photograph taken in poor light, its shadows further deprived of modelling by half-tone reproduction.

STRIPPERS

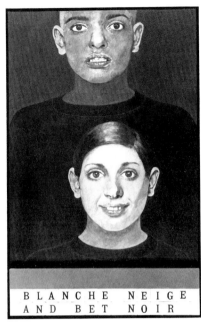

65

66

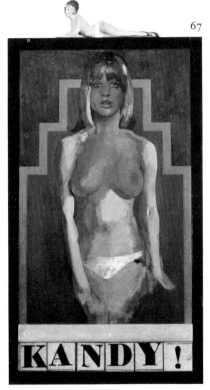

67

67 Kandy 1963–5
 Cryla and collage on hardboard
 $11\frac{1}{2} \times 6(29.2 \times 15.2)$
 Mrs Stoutzker

Begun in 1963 as an oldish stripper
'Lolita', she was given the name of the
heroine of Terry Southern's novel and
made younger in 1963 for the exhibition
at the Robert Fraser Gallery 1965. After
the photograph for that catalogue was
taken the picture was developed, especially in the face and hair. The face
has come to look more like Bardot.

68 Selina Silver 1968–77
 Oil on panel
 $9\frac{3}{4} \times 6\frac{3}{4}(24.8 \times 17.2)$
 Waddington Galleries

A fictional stripper, based on a photograph in a 'girlie' magazine. The lettering is from a children's game and the
surround is made up of coloured coun-
ters which reinforce the childlike face of
the subject.

PIN-UPS

69 Pin Up Girl 1962
 Oil on hardboard
 $19 \times 13\frac{5}{8}(48.3 \times 34.6)$
 Waddington Galleries

Painted from life. Blake used the same
model as for the figure in the upper
right corner of 'Girls with their Hero'
(Cat. no. 42).

70 Pin-up Girl 1962
 Oil on hardboard
 $9 \times 6\frac{1}{2}(23 \times 16.5)$
 Adrian Heath

This and the following number are
from photographs in 'girlie' magazines
and are intended to serve as pin-ups
without any fictional, biographical
illusions or comment.

68

71 Pin-up Girl 1965
Cryla on hardboard
$13 \times 10\frac{1}{2}(33 \times 26.7)$
Private collection, Brussels

POSTCARDS

72 Couples 1959
Collage on a notice board
$35 \times 23\frac{1}{2}(89 \times 59.7)$
Peter Blake

An early work on the theme of love and based on the kind of material Blake collected on his Leverhulme travels. The cards are old-fashioned and of a type and origin more Mediterranean than English or American. They are presented in rows on the actual notice board. The device characterises the nature of the production of such images as variations on a basic type.

69

71

73 Postcard 1961
Oil on hardboard
$48 \times 30(122 \times 76.2)$
Museums Boymans-Van
Beuningen, Rotterdam

Based on a card of Spanish or Italian origin and of the first decade of the century.

74 Postcard 1962
Oil on hardboard
$48 \times 30(122 \times 76.2)$
Waddington Galleries

Based on a card of the type collaged in 'Couples'. The iconography derives ultimately from sixteenth and seven-

73

teenth century genre painting. Blake copies the series number in the corner and exaggerates the effect of cheap printing while enlarging the scale.

75 Aparicio 1963
Oil, string and metal on hardboard
$48 \times 30(122 \times 76.2)$
Coll. Hans Sonnenberg,
Rotterdam
Courtesy: Galerie Delta,
Rotterdam

Based on a bullfighter card collected by Blake in Spain. Spanish themes appear however before Blake's visit in 1956, see 'Litter' (Cat.no.6). The dots at the top are dents and represent drawing-pin holes. The braid or frogging on the coat is string threaded through the panel.

253/12

74

75

76 Le Petit Porteur 1964–5
Cryla on hardboard
30 × 18(76.2 × 45.7)
Waddington Galleries

With Cat.no.77 derived from cards in a long series printed in Italy and published in France c.1900 called 'Salut de Constantinople'. Such subjects had novelettish associations. The painting style is close to the Pin-ups of the same date.

77 Bedouin 1964–5
Cryla on hardboard
30½ × 18¾(77.4 × 47.7)
Thyssen-Bornemisza Collection, Lugano, Switzerland

![763 Bedouin](image of painting)

77

78 Mark, Henrietta and Charlie Boxer 1965
Cryla on hardboard
14 × 12(35.6 × 30.5)
Mark Boxer

The sitter is Marc the cartoonist who, like Blake, was influenced early on by Saul Steinberg. The portrait was commissioned by *The Sunday Times* on the occasion when the sitter left to edit *London Life*. The effect of silhouetting the figures against the sky is a tribute to the illustrator Maxfield Parrish whose illustrations to Eugene Field's 'Poems of Childhood' Blake admires.

79 Simon Rodia 1965
Cryla on hardboard
12 × 14(30.5 × 35.6)
Agnes and Frits Becht, Naarden, Holland

79

Painted from a magazine picture of the maker of the Watts Towers in Los Angeles County which Blake saw in 1963. The towers are set with fragments of pottery and tile. Blake painted the passage on the left from pictures in magazines.

80 Portrait of Richard Guyatt 1981
Oil on board
$8\frac{1}{2} \times 7\frac{1}{2}(21.6 \times 19)$
Royal College of Art

Rector of the Royal College of Art 1978–1981. Commissioned by the Royal College. Painted from a series of colour photographs taken by Blake.

81 Tarzan, Jane, Boy and Cheeta 1966–75
Cryla on canvas
$48 \times 36(121.9 \times 91.5)$
Galerie Meyer-Ellinger, Frankfurt

Based on various photographs and printed images including some from body-building and 'girlie' magazines. Cheeta is from a photograph of a chimpanzee supplied by London Zoo.

The fiction is that this is a family living in Santa Monica and posing as Tarzan with his family. Father and son

are body-builders, mother equally proud of her physique. Cheeta is their pet.

The coat of arms on the wall is Blake's fictional arms of the Greystoke family to which Tarzan is supposed to have belonged in the novels of Edgar Rice Burroughs.

Blake has begun two related paintings Cat. nos. 99 and 100 and has made a number of drawings which are parallel to rather than preparatory for the paintings.

82 Monarch of the Glen 1965–8
Cryla on canvas
$48 \times 48(121.9 \times 121.9)$
Paul and Linda McCartney

Painted from a reproduction of the famous painting by Sir Edwin Landseer which has been so often used in advertisements. The subject was suggested to

82

Paul McCartney by Blake since the singer had a picture of Highland cattle which he liked. The picture by Landseer is one which, like pop stars, has an existence in the media separate from itself, and is the archetype of classical bad taste.

FAIRIES AND RURALIST WORKS

83 Puck, Peaseblossom, Cobweb, Moth and Mustard seed 1969–83
Cryla on hardboard
$39\frac{1}{2} \times 30\frac{5}{8}(100.3 \times 77.8)$
Waddington Galleries

Painted from a variety of sources. The face of the boy is Del Shannon, a pop star. This picture is related thematically to several paintings and drawings deriving equally from the inspiration of *A Midsummer Night's Dream*: Titania and Oberon.

84   Titania 1972–4
   Oil on board
   $7 \times 4\frac{5}{8}(17.8 \times 11.8)$
   Private collection, London

Blake exhibited watercolours of Oberon
and Titania at the Robert Fraser
Gallery 1969. This was his first Titania
in oil and a good example of his characterisation by the head only without
other attributes except the frame.

   He has also painted a 'Titania's
Birthday' in watercolour (Cat. no. 171)
and a 'Titania Queen of the Fairies',
now lost (Waddington Galleries 1977
no. 21).

85   Titania 1976–83
   Oil on canvas
   $48 \times 36(121.9 \times 91.4)$
   Waddington Galleries

Exhibited and reproduced at an earlier
stage of development at the Academy in
1976 and in the *Hayward Annual*, June
1977. It has since been transformed.
The body has become rather fuller, the
face broader and wilder, the hair, which
before looked like that of an ancient
Egyptian goddess, is now disarranged
and pulled back off the face and shoulders. Stems of daisies have been woven
into her less abundant pubic hair. The
lesser fairies round her feet have been
entirely changed and one now appears
above her head where there were glow-
ing lights.

   The theme of Oberon and Titania
was treated by Fuseli and William
Blake. Peter Blake knew the work of
Noel Paton the nineteenth-century
painter who exhibited a 'Quarrel' and a
'Reconciliation of Oberon and Titania'
in a classical style, 1846–7. A follower,
John Simmons, produced a number of
more obviously erotic, though still neo-
classical Titanias in the third quarter of
the nineteenth century, but this obscure
artist was not known to Blake.

87

86   Ophelia 1977–83
   Oil on hardboard
   $54\frac{3}{4} \times 38\frac{1}{8}(139.1 \times 96.8)$
   Peter Blake

Painted from life for the Ruralists'
Ophelia exhibition at Trinity College,
Cambridge and left unfinished. It has
been worked on in 1980 and 1982–3.
Blake has taken some photographs of
the model but these have not yet been
used. The moment depicted is one that
is interpolated into Shakespeare's text.
Ophelia is shown having managed to get
to her feet in the stream in which she
was to drown *(Hamlet* Act IV, scene 7)
still clutching twigs that she imagines
to be the flowers that she speaks of in
Act IV, scene 5, rosemary, pansies,
fennel, columbines, rue, daisies and
violets.

**87   Rossweisse – Fairy
   Warrior** 1977
   Oil on hardboard
   $10 \times 8(25.4 \times 20.3)$
   Waddington Galleries

The objects strung round her neck and
arm are a mixture of natural and man-
made decorations found by her. They
include a vulcanite screw bottle-
stopper, a conker, a sea-shell and two
objects made of leaves and flowers by
Liberty and Daisy Blake.

   The idea of showing only the lower
half of the face goes back to cat. no. 7a.

88   Flora–Fairy Child 1977
   Oil on hardboard
   $6\frac{1}{4} \times 4\frac{1}{2}(15.9 \times 11.4)$
   Private collection

The face is developed from a picture in
a magazine of a girl named, coinciden-
tally, Florence. Blake made the coronet
of flowers and photographed it. The
italianate frame is suited to the fairy
named after a Roman Goddess.

   In this series generally the frames are
matched with the subject of the picture
at an early stage and form part of its

88

90

91 **Fairy with Toadstools** ?1977
Oil on hardboard
$5\frac{1}{2} \times 4 (14 \times 10.1)$
Private collection

Image from a 'girlie' magazine with details from nature. The carved oak frame was found.

92 **Eglentyne** 1981–2
Oil on hardboard
$3\frac{1}{2} \times 3\frac{1}{2} (8.9 \times 8.9)$
Waddington Galleries

The frame here is in a baroque style rather contrasting with the plain head and neck.

93 **Fairy Child Crying** 1981–2
Oil on canvas
$6 \times 6 (15.2 \times 15.2)$
Galleria Forni, Bologna

Based on a picture from a photograph in the magazine *Nova*, with a tear and oak leaves added.

94 **Daisy Fairy** 1981–2
Oil on hardboard
$4\frac{5}{8} \times 2\frac{1}{2} (11.7 \times 6.3)$
Waddington Galleries

apparatus of characterisation just like the badges in the wrestlers. They are often large or elaborate in relation to the painting like those of the madonna painters of the fifteenth century. Most of the frames would have had only a small print, photograph or reproduction in them so the presence of the exquisitely painted heads that look out at one is startling and draws attention. The discrepancy of medium and similarity of content between frame and picture is analogous to his method in pictures of all kinds but is more concise than in most.

89 **Dolores–Fairy Girl** 1977
Oil on hardboard
$5\frac{3}{4} \times 4\frac{1}{2} (14.6 \times 11.4)$
Peter Blake

90 **Placida–Fairy Child** 1977
Oil on hardboard
$9 \times 8 (22.9 \times 20.3)$
Everard Read collection

Based on a photograph of a child in an Avianca advertisement to which Blake has added a chestnut husk as a hat. The frame is found, perhaps late nineteenth century. It is similar to a kind sometimes found on religious images but also on samplers and mottoes.

91

93

94

Based on a magazine picture. The carved frame is in an asiatic style, the necklace of daisy stalks or grasses; both are rather homely.

95 Poppy Fairy 1981–2
Oil on hardboard
6 × 5(15.2 × 12.7)
Private collection

Based on a magazine photograph with poppy added. As in all cases, the expression is subtly changed, very often by slightly enlarging and emphasising the features. The frame is Netherlandish in type, made specially by Robert Sielle.

96 Nadia 1981
Oil on hardboard
11½ × 8½(29.2 × 20.3)
Richard Brown Baker

Given marine associations, perhaps from the similarity of the name to Naiad although the name is Russian signifying 'hope'.

**97 The Owl and the
Pussycat** 1981–3
Oil on hardboard
10¾ × 12½(27.3 × 31.8)
The City of Bristol Museum and
Art Gallery

Made to fit the embossed copper frame from which the shape of the boat is derived. The work illustrates literally the poem of Lear:

'The Owl and the Pussycat went to sea
In a beautiful Pea-green boat.
They took some honey
And plenty of money
Wrapped up in a five-pound note'

THE DEFINITIVE NUDE

Following the showing of their Ophelia paintings in 1980, the members of the Brotherhood of Ruralists agreed to paint what was for each of them 'The Definitive Nude'. They were all to be on canvases of identical size and to be shown together.

Peter Blake
98a The Wedding Hat 1981–3
Oil on canvas
68½ × 48(174 × 121.9)
Peter Blake

Painted from specially taken photographs. This is almost a straightforward life painting in a modern interior and with relatively little narrative suggestion. The pose is close to that of ancient Greek or pre-classical Greek statues but also that of a person posing in the most straightforward way possible.

Ann Arnold
98b Miranda 1982
Oil on canvas
68½ × 48(174 × 121.9)
The artist

98a

Graham Arnold
98c Janet Millar and the Milky Way 1982
Oil on canvas
$68\frac{1}{2} \times 48(174 \times 121.9)$
The artist

David Inshaw
98d Beatrice Phillpots 1982
Oil on canvas
$68\frac{1}{2} \times 48(174 \times 121.9)$
Waddington Galleries

Annie Ovenden
98e On the Dunes 1982
Oil on canvas
$68\frac{1}{2} \times 48(174 \times 121.9)$
The artist

Graham Ovenden
98f Elinor 1982
Oil on canvas
$68\frac{1}{2} \times 48(174 \times 121.9)$
Waddington and Piccadilly Galleries

PAINTINGS IN PROGRESS

99 Tarzan meets the Jungle Goddess
Cryla on canvas
$36 \times 48(91.4 \times 121.9)$
Peter Blake

A painting made in parallel with the watercolours (Cat. nos 150–151) and on a theme related to Cat. no. 81. The composition reverts to the type of the group snapshot which seems at first to be at variance with the subject.

100 Tarzan and his family at the Roxy Cinema, New York
begun 1965
Cryla on canvas
$72 \times 60(182.9 \times 152.4)$
Peter Blake

This picture, one of several Tarzans, was painted in a large studio that Blake rented in 1965 specially to paint three big pictures; this, the portrait of David Hockney and 'Sword Fight'. All remain unfinished. Blake made a point of showing unfinished work also at the Hayward Gallery in 1971

101 Sword Fight begun 1965
Cryla on canvas
$72 \times 112(182.9 \times 284.5)$
Peter Blake

The picture is a stage set and at the same time a table top on which a game has been set out. It is based on the clichéd theme of the pantomime and cinema sword fight. Originally the Baddies were wrestlers and the Goodies movie stars like Fairbanks and other manly heroes. At the time of writing the figures are very vague and may be realised in more modern terms with reference to new painting just as the Sculpture Park refers to sculptural types.

102 Portrait of David Hockney in a Hollywood-Spanish Interior begun 1965 and worked on intermittently
Cryla on canvas
$72 \times 60(182.9 \times 152.4)$
David Hockney

The background is derived from a magazine photograph which was enlarged so that Hockney could be photographed in front of it. Details like the balloons, confetti and streamers come from other sources. The confetti and streamers were also considered for 'Tarzan at the Roxy Cinema'.

103 A Mad Tea Party at Watts Tower c.1968
Oil on canvas
$36 \times 48(91.4 \times 121.9)$
Peter Blake

This is a composite picture derived from a number of sources. Alice is from a ballet dancer of the 50s. The Mad Hatter is based on an advertisement but his face is from a german portrait photograph. Photographs from the zoo were used for the hare and the dormouse. The background of the Watts Tower was put together and elaborated from magazine pictures etc. A drawing of the same subject is Cat. no. 208.

[103]

CALIFORNIAN PICTURES

Blake and Hodgkin agreed to paint three pictures each, recalling their visit to Los Angeles at a time when both were pondering the reconstruction of their way of life. David Hockney, who was living there, acted as host and cicerone.

Peter Blake
104 Montgomery Clift was a Twin 1981–3
From a photograph by Kevin McCarthy 'At Paestum, an old Greek Colony south of Naples'.
Oval, oil on canvas
35 × 26¾(88.9 × 68)
Peter Blake

Like nos 105 and 106 below, this recalls a visit to Los Angeles in the company of Howard Hodgkin (see Cat.nos. 104a, 105a and 106a). The strange, pale shape behind his head is a handkerchief tucked into the frame of his dark glasses to shade his neck. Blake was reading his biography in Los Angeles. The frame is

a rather decayed Victorian one in gilt composition, like those of the other two Hollywood pictures.

Howard Hodgkin
104a David's Swimming Pool 1982
Mixed media on paper
24½ × 31¼(62.3 × 79.4)
The artist

Peter Blake
105 'The Meeting' or 'Have a nice day, Mr Hockney' 1981–3
Oil on canvas
38½ × 48¾(97.8 × 123.8)
Peter Blake

The picture is an updating of Courbet's 'The Meeting' alias 'Bonjour Monsieur Courbet', in a Los Angeles setting. David Hockney is Courbet, Blake Monsieur Bruyas, Courbet's patron, and Howard Hodgkin plays the role of Bruyas' servant. The bravado of Courbet who took his composition from a popular print of 'The Wandering Jew' becomes a play of irony as the three artists meet. It is Hockney who is on his own ground in real life and Hodgkin who had begun to argue openly for the recognition of the artist's importance. Hockney's staff has become a brush, an echo of Daumier's cartoon of the battle of the styles. The background is the boulevard near the beach where roller skaters abound. Some figures are drawn from photographs especially taken on a later visit. The girl squatting in

105

the foreground is from the cover of a skating magazine, just as the wrestlers were drawn from their own magazine medium. The composition is different from most of Blake's, going back beyond Courbet to the Italian Renaissance. The central group is supported by more distant figures mainly aligned along a diagonal that runs across the parallel horizontals of the setting. As in many such pictures, one of the figures is looking out at the viewer and she almost completely distracts the eye from the main group, just as one may in a family group photo.

Howard Hodgkin
105a David Hockney in Hollywood 1982
Oil on wood
$42\frac{1}{2} \times 51\frac{1}{2}(108 \times 130.8)$
The artist

Peter Blake
106 A Remembered Moment in Venice, Cal. 1981–3
Oil on canvas
$31\frac{1}{4} \times 41\frac{1}{2}(79.4 \times 105.4)$
Peter Blake

As Peter Blake and Howard Hodgkin were walking back from the beach to a gallery they saw a teenaged girl day-dreaming on her skates by a parking lot. When Blake went back he could not find the space, for it had been transformed into a new building and there was a new parking lot in the next block. The figure in the painting is now that of Daisy Blake.

Howard Hodgkin
106a Deja Vous 1982
Oil on panel
$35 \times 51(88.9 \times 129.5)$
The artist

COLLAGE

107 Dutch Collage 1956
Collage
$6\frac{1}{8} \times 8\frac{1}{2}(15.6 \times 21.6)$
Peter Blake

This collage and the following one were made of materials collected in Europe on Blake's travels 1956–7.

108 Metallic papers collage 1956
Collage
$6 \times 7\frac{3}{4}(15.2 \times 19.7)$
Peter Blake

109 Collage 1957
Collage
$9\frac{3}{4} \times 12(24.7 \times 30.5)$
Ian Kennedy Martin

110 Jockey Act 1957
Collage
$28\frac{1}{2} \times 34\frac{1}{4}(72.4 \times 87)$
Erik and Lilott Bergamus

One of a number of figurative collages made by Blake under the influence of

110

Ernst and Schwitters between the abstract collages of 1956 and the appearance of his own collage style exemplified in 'Girlie Door' (Cat. no. 39). Most were given away like the later 'Souvenirs'. He was to return to something like the manner of Jockey Act in the mid 70s. See also Cat. nos 109 and 111.

111 Bird Act 1957
Collage
$9\frac{5}{8} \times 14\frac{1}{4}(24.5 \times 36.2)$
·Waddington Galleries

A 'circus act' dedicated with apologies to Saul Steinberg. The birds are made up of worn metal shoe heels.

112 A Museum for Myself 1982
Collage
$45\frac{3}{8} \times 33\frac{7}{8}(115.3 \times 86)$
Peter Blake

A collection of objects some of which refer to art. However, they are essentially things that Blake has collected and likes. In this respect they resemble 'Toy Shop' (Cat. no. 37). In composition it is closer to Medals (Cat. no. 27).

SOUVENIRS

Text from Waddington Galleries catalogue 1977:

'The first two souvenirs were made in 1968 as my contribution to Aspen 7 'British Box'. Souvenir No. 3 was given to David Hockney, and then the series continued spasmodically. In 1974 my wife Jann Haworth and I were invited by the Festival Gallery in Bath to put on an exhibition for the Bath Festival. For this I made a further thirty souvenirs. They were made to be given to the person to whom each is dedicated.'

Drawings that he gave to friends and the collages of 1956–7 were the forerunners of the Souvenirs.

113

113 Souvenir for Judith 1973
Collage
$9\frac{3}{4} \times 7\frac{1}{4}(24.8 \times 18.4)$
Judith Elliott

The first souvenir of the main series beginning in 1973.

114 Souvenir for John (Lennon) 1973
Collage
$12 \times 8\frac{7}{8}(30.5 \times 22.5)$
Peter Blake

John Lennon, singer and composer 1940 to 1980.

The reference is to a phrase in the song 'For the benefit of Mr Kite' from the record 'Sergeant Pepper's Lonely Hearts Club Band' (see Cat. no. 226). Blake made two attempts to deliver the souvenir to John Lennon in New York but was unable to make contact with him.

115 Souvenir for Jim Dine 1974
Collage
$14 \times 20\frac{1}{8}(35.6 \times 51.1)$
Jim Dine

Jim Dine, American artist, regular visitor to England. In his early works he made frequent use of tools. The two pages illustrate ranges of garden tools *c*.1910 from a scrap book.

116 Souvenir for Hockney 1974
Collage
$11\frac{3}{4} \times 13\frac{7}{8}(29.8 \times 35.2)$
David Hockney

Hockney, as the dedication implies, had been living in Paris. Apparently not the Souvenir mentioned in the text at the head of this section.

117 Souvenir for Gilbert and George 1974
Collage
$17\frac{3}{4} \times 9\frac{3}{4}(45.1 \times 24.7)$
Gilbert and George

Bud Flanagan and Chesney Allen were the music hall stars who made the song 'Underneath the Arches' famous. Gilbert and George's work of the same name uses a recording by other voices.

118 Souvenir for Joe 1974
$18 \times 18\frac{1}{4} \times 2(45.7 \times 46.3 \times 5)$
Private collection

Joe Tilson artist, contemporary with Blake.

118

The allusion is to the numerous works made in wood by Tilson who was trained as a carpenter.

119 Souvenir for Jos 1974
$9\frac{1}{2} \times 6\frac{1}{2} \times \frac{3}{4}(24.1 \times 16.5 \times 1.9)$
Private collection

Jos is the wife of Joe Tilson. The Tilsons have a house not far from Wellow where Blake lived.

120 Souvenir for Kitaj 1974
Collage
$46\frac{3}{4} \times 18\frac{1}{4}(118.8 \times 46.4)$
R. B. Kitaj

R. B. Kitaj, the American painter working in London, was a student at the Royal College just after Blake, 1960–62, and a protagonist of figure painting. He came from Cleveland and had been a baseball fan.

121 Souvenir for Gordon House 1974–5
Collage
$11 \times 12\frac{1}{4}(28 \times 31)$
Gordon and Jo House

The geese appear to be a modern Chinese print.

119

121

122 Souvenir for Daisy 1974
Collage
$5\frac{3}{4} \times 3\frac{1}{2}(14.6 \times 8.9)$
Daisy Blake

Daisy Blake is the artist's younger daughter born in 1974.

123 A Little Museum for Tom Phillips 1977
Collage
$15\frac{1}{4} \times 9\frac{1}{2}(38.7 \times 24.2)$
Tom Phillips

Tom Phillips the painter. Several of his works depict works of art in a museum setting.

SCULPTURE

124 Fragments from 'Crazy said Snow White' 1959
Various media and sizes
Peter Blake

The title of this group comes from a Stan Freberg record. The whole work was exhibited at the ICA in 1960; only a few elements were saved. They include part of an etruscan terracotta head, a Spanish clown, a now headless Indian figure and a head and shoulders made of two bits of found stone.

125

125 Superman Figure, detail from 'Crazy said Snow-White' 1959
Painted metal sculpture
$16 \times 13 \times 6(40.6 \times 33 \times 15.2)$
Mr and Mrs Robert Melville

The group is an altered ornament based on one of the 'Horsetamers' of the Quirinale in Rome and thought to be Castor and Pollux. Superman has been substituted for one of the Greek Gods. Small copies were very popular in the nineteenth and earlier twentieth centuries.

126 Locker 1959
Mixed media
$60 \times 30 \times 30(152.4 \times 76.2 \times 76.2)$
Peter Blake

An RAF locker that had been painted blue. Blake decorated it with collages of film stars, jazz and rock singers, pin-ups etc. They include Kim Novak, Brigitte Bardot, Sammy Davis Jr., the Dave Brubeck quartet, Mister World, Dean Martin, the Hell's Angels, Pier Angeli, Mai Britt, Elsa Martinelli, Jayne Mansfield, Marilyn Monroe, Laurel and Hardy.

127 Pair of Painted Shoes, detail from 'Locker' 1959
Enamels on wood
$10\frac{3}{4} \times 9 \times 8\frac{1}{4}(27.3 \times 22.9 \times 21)$
Peter Blake

A pair of shoe-trees, without the heel element, painted in the fashion of two-tone brogues called 'Co-respondent's' shoes.
Exhibited first (ICA 1960). They were inside the Locker, cat. no. 126.

128 Drum Majorette c.1959
Oil and collage on dressmaker's dummy
$35 \times 23 \times 40(88.9 \times 58.4 \times 101.6)$
Peter Blake

127

Related to cat. nos 26 and 27 and exhibited with 'Crazy said Snow White'. Paul McCartney added a medal to it.

129 Bodhisattva sculpture 1959–60
Found pieces of wood and gilt painted
$17 \times 4\frac{3}{4} \times 3(43.1 \times 12 \times 7.6)$
Peter Blake

Made at the same time as the Japanese influenced gold pictures and referring to Japanese Zen Buddhism as promoted by Kerouac and the 'Beat generation' in, for example, the former's *Dharma Bums*.

130 Man meeting a Tiger on a Bridge 1960
Painted wood
$7\frac{3}{8} \times 11\frac{1}{2} \times 2\frac{3}{4}(18.7 \times 29.2 \times 7)$
Peter Blake

The forerunner of several recent sculptures related to the 'Sculpture Park' (Cat. no. 137)

131 Three Man Up c.1960
Metal and wood
$11 \times 1\frac{3}{4} \times 2\frac{1}{4}(28 \times 4.5 \times 5.7)$
Private collection

An oriental figure surmounted by two metal figures of strong-men on a

131

134

different scale. Blake used an identical strong-man much later as Stuart Brisley in 'Sculpture Park' (Cat. no. 137). The term three man up is used to describe a column of three people in a circus act.

132 Captain Webb Matchbox c.1960–61
Gouache and pencil on wood and hardboard
$15\frac{3}{4} \times 11\frac{7}{16} \times 4\frac{1}{8}$ (40 × 29 × 10.5)
Private collection

A box painted to simulate a matchbox. Captain Webb was credited with the first swimming of the English Channel. The idea of a box once again anticipated Warhol.

133 Figure on a Box c.1961
Wood, brick
$56\frac{3}{4} \times 9 \times 8\frac{1}{2}$ (144.1 × 22.8 × 21.6)
Peter Blake

A column of bricks and pieces of wood. These figures are much more dead-pan than the rather earlier and contem-

132

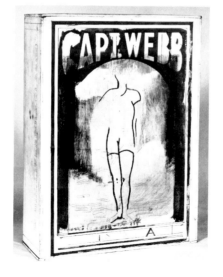

porary works of assemblage artists. They have a quality of play and resemble the most simple figures made by children as well as those produced by certain primitives. Blake has returned to this way of working in the 80s.
(Cat. nos 135 and 136)

134 Tarzan Box c.1965
Mixed media
$14\frac{1}{2} \times 22\frac{1}{2} \times 12$ (36.8 × 57.1 × 30.5)
Peter Blake

This is a tableau based on features of the Tarzan story: the crashed plane in which Jane arrives in the jungle, Jane with impeccable dress and hair, a black Chief in a Hollywood idea of war costume, Tarzan entering swinging on a piece of string simulating a liana or vine.

[109]

135 Boy, Girl and Horse 1982
Iron and marble
$3\frac{7}{8} \times 5\frac{1}{4} \times 3 (9.8 \times 13.3 \times 7.6)$
Waddington Galleries

The work is on a marble base which was supplied as a sample for a bathroom. The three pieces of rusty iron were found on the beach by Liberty Blake on a visit to Lyme Regis.

136 Incident in an Art Gallery 1982
Marble, ivory, china, wood
$4\frac{1}{4} \times 5\frac{1}{4} \times 5 (10.8 \times 13.3 \times 12.7)$
Private collection

A sculpture loosely on the theme of visitors to a gallery being themselves works of art represented by found objects. They include an eastern ivory figure and an ivory lion, two china babies of the type known as 'Frozen Charlottes', a 'Dirty Gertie' and two pipe bowls on little sculpture bases.

137 Sculpture Park 1981–3
Mixed media
$96 \times 144 (244 \times 365.5)$
Peter Blake

This work comprises manufactured objects which have been found or purchased; natural, found objects (items in both categories may have been adjusted or painted); with specially constructed objects, sometimes made of manufactured materials. Some of the objects were collected many years ago, before the concept of the work was clearly formulated, others have been collected more recently to fit into the evolving scheme. The idea is a development of that of 'Crazy said Snow White', 1960. Most of the construction of 'Sculpture Park' has been carried out by Chrissy Wilson.

There will also be a group of sculptures, entitled 'Incident from a Sculpture Park'.

WATERCOLOURS AND GOUACHE

138 Fairground Booths *c*.1950
Gouache and watercolour
$14\frac{3}{4} \times 21 (37.5 \times 53.3)$
Peter Blake

An early example of Blake's interest in the fairground and circus. The convention of drawing horizontal and vertical surfaces in the same plane is similar to that in paintings like 'Preparation for the Entry into Jerusalem' (Cat.no.9).

139 Boy with New Tie *c*.1951–3
Pen and ink and gouache on paper
$6\frac{1}{2} \times 5\frac{1}{2} (16.5 \times 14)$
Private collection

Essentially a self-portrait drawn from a family snapshot. This is a typical early figure composition, having a distant landscape in the manner of fifteenth-century Italian and Flemish portraits. The boy is showing off his adult dark glasses and sexy tie 'Miss CWS' (Co-operative Wholesale Society). Blake

painted his own ties while at Gravesend. Among many textures used by Blake are numerous hand or finger prints in the paint.

**140 Self Portrait
(In RAF Jacket)** *c*.1952–3
Pen and ink and gouache on paper
$13\frac{1}{2} \times 9\frac{1}{4} (34.2 \times 23.5)$
Private collection

Painted during his period of national service, 1951–3. This watercolour establishes one of Blake's favourite compositions, the half-length frontal pose as for a photograph.

He is wearing Harlequin trousers and a singlet over which is thrown an RAF jacket. The trousers and the background of circus posters contrast his own interests with the demands of the services. At this time Blake was rather self-conscious about his appearance having a deep scar on his face as a result of a cycling accident. This was covered up by the beard which he has worn unchanged almost ever since.

141 Tattooed Lady I 1955
Pen, ink, gouache and collage on paper
21 × 14(53.2 × 35.5)
Robyn Denny

In this instance the tattooed designs are taken from a book in the Victoria and Albert Museum on French criminal tattoos.

142 Tattooed Lady with Collage 1958
Gouache and collage
27 × 21(68.6 × 53.3)
Victoria and Albert Museum, London

The body of the lady is covered with scraps rather in the manner of a Victorian screen. Many of these are of European origin and may have been collected on Blake's travels. The collaged area is set off to the right in relation to the outline – an early example of Blake imitating the effect of bad registration from cheap printing.

143 Tattooed Lady 1961
Pen and wash on paper
37¼ × 20⅝(94.6 × 52.4)
Gordon and Jo House

A variety of images from nineteenth- and twentieth-century imprints including Elvis and the name Bo Diddley.

144 Butcher Cottage Summer 1967 1967
Watercolour and pencil on paper
9 × 16(22.9 × 40.7)
Miriam Haworth

Drawn from nature in Surrey. Although Blake had used gouache, which is water-soluble, from his earliest days he took up the traditional medium of watercolour only in 1967.

145 April in a Dressing Gown 1968
Watercolour and pencil on paper
45½ × 32½(115.6 × 82.5)
Annelotte Elbrecht, Frankfurt

April Wilson was Blake's half sister-in-law; she lived in London.

146 April in a Kimono 1968
Watercolour
25 × 20½(63.5 × 52.1)
Private collection

147 James Joyce as a Young Man 1969
Watercolour on paper
14 × 11 (35.6 × 28)
Private collection

James Joyce aged twenty-two drawn from a photograph.

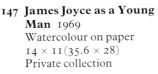

146

Drawn on the same occasion as cat. no. 145. Apparently in the same robe. See also cat. no. 202 'April with Pipalo and Star King'.

147

148 Girl in a Poppy Field 1968–9
Watercolour on paper
16 × 11 (40.6 × 29.2)
Private collection

The artist bought a new box of watercolours and the central diagonal area was an experiment with them which he turned into a knitted multi-coloured jacket.

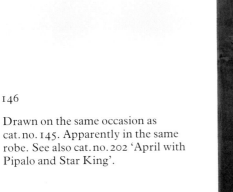

149 Boy eating Water Melon 1969
Watercolour
14 × 12 (35.6 × 30.5)
San Lorenzo Restaurant

Related in concept to the painting 'Boy with Hot Dog' (Cat. no. 20).

150 Study for Tarzan meets Jungle Goddess II 1969
Watercolour
$5\frac{1}{2} \times 3\frac{3}{4}$ (14 × 9.5)
Private collection

In an Indian or East African frame of carved wood and mother-of-pearl.

Blake drew a series of African heads in preparation for the unfinished picture of this name, probably from documentary photographs in the *National Geographic Magazine*.

151 Jane and Cheeta 1969
Watercolour
11 × 9 (28 × 22.9)
Private collection

Cheeta is drawn from a London Zoo photograph.

150

151

152 Study of Streamers and Confetti *c.*1969
Watercolour
$23\frac{1}{2} \times 18(59.7 \times 45.7)$; with two attached frames containing respectively streamers and confetti, each $2\frac{3}{4} \times 2\frac{3}{4}(7 \times 7)$
Waddington Galleries

Studies for the 'Portrait of David Hockney' begun in 1965. Blake also used confetti in studies for 'Jane and Cheeta'.

153 Illustration to Through the Looking-Glass
'So Alice picked him up very gently' 1970–71
Watercolour
Image size $10 \times 8(25.4 \times 20.3)$;
paper size $26 \times 21(66 \times 53.3)$
Deweer Art Gallery, Zwevegem-Otegem, Belgium

Blake planned to illustrate *Through the Looking Glass* while Graham Ovenden did *Alice in Wonderland*, for a proposed new edition of the books. However, the project was never realised and the artists contented themselves with sets of prints. Blake read the book several times as a preparation for the series. On a visit to Holland he read passages to Amelia Gatacre and asked her to enact scenes, directing as if making a film. Then photographs were taken and used in making the watercolours. Blake has either illustrated scenes as described or tried to fill in, convincingly, moments in the minute gaps of the narrative using his imagination and trying to avoid following Tenniel. However, sometimes a Tenniel idea is taken and deliberately varied. Other parts were realised from photographs but the landscapes were drawn from nature in the environs of Wellow or in Holland.

154 Illustration to Through the Looking-Glass
'"It isn't manners for us to begin, you know", said the Rose' 1970–71
Watercolour
Image size $10 \times 8(25.4 \times 20.3)$;
paper size $26 \times 21(66 \times 53.3)$
Private collection

155 Illustration to Through the Looking-Glass
'Just at this moment, somehow or other, they began to run' 1970–71
Watercolour
Image size $10 \times 8(25.4 \times 20.3)$;
paper size $26 \times 21(66 \times 53.3)$
Private collection

156 Illustration to Through the Looking-Glass
'"But it isn't old!" Tweedledum cried' 1970–71
Watercolour
Image size $10 \times 8(25.4 \times 20.3)$;
paper size $26 \times 21(66 \times 53.3)$
Private collection

157 Illustration to Through the Looking-Glass 'and to show you I'm not proud, you may shake hands with me!' 1970–71
Watercolour
Image size 10 × 8(25.4 × 20.3);
paper size 26 × 21(66 × 53.3)
Private collection

158 Illustration to Through the Looking-Glass 'For instance, now there's the King's messenger' 1970–71
Watercolour
Image size 10 × 8(25.4 × 20.3);
paper size 26 × 21(66 × 53.3)
Private collection

159 Illustration to Through the Looking-Glass 'and the two Knights sat, and looked at each other without speaking' 1970–71
Watercolour
Image size 10 × 8(25.4 × 20.3);
paper size 26 × 21(66 × 53.3)
Deweer Art Gallery, Zwevegem-Otegem, Belgium

160 Illustration to Through the Looking-Glass '"Well this is grand!" said Alice' 1970–71
Watercolour
Image size 10 × 8(25.4 × 20.3);
paper size 26 × 21(66 × 53.3)
Private collection

161 Liberty Blake in a Kimono 1971
Watercolour
Private collection

Drawn at Wellow for a Habitat reproduction. Juliette Liberty Blake, the artist's elder daughter, was born in 1968.

162 To Jann on Mother's Day 1971
Watercolour
$11\frac{1}{8}$ × 8(28.2 × 20.3)
Private collection

A posy of flowers collected by Liberty Blake.

163

163 Flowers in a Vase, or a Posy for Liberty 1972
Watercolour
9 × $7\frac{1}{2}$(22.9 × 19)
Private collection

In a cork frame, the flowers were picked by Liberty Blake.

164

164 The Tuareg 1972
Watercolour
18 × $11\frac{3}{4}$(45.7 × 29.8)
Anya and Laura Waddington

One of a series, Cat. nos 165–168, drawn as imaginary national types of wrestler, they were made into silkscreen prints, Waddington Galleries, 1972.

165 Red Power 1972
Watercolour
18 × 11¾(45.7 × 29.8)
Anya and Laura Waddington

166 Pretty Boy Michael Angelo 1972
Watercolour
18 × 11¾(45.7 × 29.8)
Anya and Laura Waddington

Drawn from a news picture of a skinhead.

167 Ebony Tarzan 1972
Watercolour
18 × 11¾(45.7 × 29.8)
Anya and Laura Waddington

168 Penny Black 1972
Watercolour
18 × 11¾(45.7 × 29.8)
Anya and Laura Waddington

169 Jeune Fille Morocaine 1972
Watercolour
5½ × 3½(14 × 8.9)
Private collection

In an Indian or East African frame drawn from a postcard.

170 Fiona Grant 1973 in progress 1977
Watercolour
9¼ × 7¼(23.5 × 18.4)
Mrs Neville Burston

The sitter is a friend of the artist from Edinburgh.

172

175

171 Titania's Birthday 1975
Watercolour
$22\frac{3}{4} \times 15\frac{1}{2}$ (57.8 × 39.4)
Museum Boymans–Van
Beuningen, Rotterdam

Related to the paintings (Cat. nos 84
and 85). The heads include those of
Pete Townshend of The Who and
various actors.

172 Ford Cottage, Coombe 1976
Watercolour
$16\frac{1}{2} \times 10\frac{1}{4}$ (41.9 × 26)
Private collection

Coombe is on the north coast of
Cornwall. Painted on his annual visit to
Coombe with the Ruralists. The
Ruralists stayed in cottages owned by
the Landmark Trust every autumn
until 1980.

173 Flowers at Coombe 1977
Watercolour
$16\frac{1}{8} \times 10\frac{1}{4}$ (41 × 26)
Private collection

174 Study for Puck 1977
Watercolour and gouache
$14\frac{1}{2} \times 11$ (37 × 27.8)
Her Majesty The Queen. Royal
Library, Windsor Castle

Given to the Queen by the Royal
Academy in 1977 as part of their Silver
Jubilee gift.

175 Pretty Penny 1977
Gouache and collage
$5\frac{1}{2} \times 4\frac{1}{8}$ (14 × 10.5)
Waddington Galleries

An imaginary black wrestler. The two
girls at the top appear to be Indian.

**176 Bernie Berni – Jewish/Italian
Mat Star** 1977
Watercolour
$3 \times 15\frac{7}{8}$ (7.6 × 40.3)
Private collection

177

In Tunbridge Wells ware frame.

The name is a kind of pun on two spellings, one commonly a Jewish nickname, the other that of Lorenzo Berni a restaurateur, collector and friend of the artist.

177 Hollywood Blondes versus the Gilded Sluts 1977
Watercolour
$3 \times 5\frac{7}{8}(7.6 \times 14.9)$
Peter Blake

A fictional 'gay' male tag team. The second head from the left was drawn from a picture of a skinhead.

178 Demolition Squad, Birmingham Drizzle and the Lady Doctor versus the Nice Girls
Watercolour and collage
$2\frac{1}{2} \times 12\frac{1}{4}(6.3 \times 31.1)$
Galerie Meyer-Ellinger

A fictional 'gay' female tag team.

179 Calendar *c.*1977–in progress
Watercolour and lithographed card
$11\frac{1}{2} \times 8\frac{1}{2}(29.2 \times 21.6)$
Peter Blake

The twelve mounts incorporated into this work are the pages of a Victorian photograph album decorated in chromolithography with birds and flowers representing the months. Blake has inserted drawings of fairies suiting the mood of the month.

180 Costume Life Drawing 1979
Watercolour
$16\frac{3}{4} \times 8\frac{7}{8}(42.6 \times 22.5)$
Paul E. Johnen

The exotic costume was collected by Blake.

180

181 Girl in a Mask 1981
Watercolour
$16 \times 10\frac{1}{8}(40.6 \times 25.7)$
Peter Blake

Painted for an exhibition of masks. The sitter is Chrissy Wilson wearing a party mask of the sort sold for Christmas.

DRAWINGS

182 Fish shop *c.*1947–8
Pencil
$4\frac{1}{2} \times 5\frac{1}{2}(11.4 \times 14)$
Peter Blake

Done while Blake was studying illustration at Gravesend. An early manifes-

181

tation of the rectilinearly divided composition combining people, objects and pattern he developed in the early 60s.

183 Conversation *c.*1948
Pencil, $6\frac{1}{2} \times 5\frac{1}{2}(16.5 \times 14)$
Peter Blake

This early composition, executed in the manner of an illustration and used as the design for a lithograph, shows the first stage of Blake's development of the theme of the environment marked with the signs of his delight in the world of fringe entertainers.

184 Bunty, St Cyr, Exciting Feather Dancer 1954
Pencil and feathers on paper
$6\frac{5}{8} \times 4\frac{7}{8}(17 \times 12.5)$
Erich Sommer

A drawing related to paintings of the type of Cat. nos 21–22.

185 Portrait, Royal College of Art 1954
Pencil on paper
$7\frac{3}{4} \times 9\frac{7}{8}(19.7 \times 25.1)$
Robert Fraser Gallery, London

This drawing and the following three are of the type done at the Royal College when the studio was so packed that Blake could not see the model. He drew the students instead.

186 Man drawing, Royal College of Art 1954
Pen and ink on paper
$7\frac{1}{4} \times 7(18.4 \times 17.8)$
Robert Fraser Gallery, London

187 Man with Glasses 1956
Pencil on paper
$5\frac{1}{8} \times 6\frac{5}{8}(13 \times 16.8)$
Robert Fraser Gallery, London

184

188 Life drawing, Royal College of Art 1956
Pencil on paper
$8 \times 5\frac{1}{4}(20.3 \times 13.3)$
Brian Clarke

189 Cafe at the Hague 1956
Pencil on paper
$6\frac{5}{8} \times 5\frac{1}{8}(16.8 \times 13)$
Robert Fraser Gallery, London

This drawing and the following five were made on Blake's European tour on the Leverhulme award.

190 Sacré Coeur 1956
Pencil on paper
$8\frac{7}{8} \times 5\frac{7}{8}(22.8 \times 14.6)$
Waddington Galleries

A figure appears to have been erased from the steps.

191 Nice 1957
Pen and ink on paper
$9\frac{5}{8} \times 13(24.5 \times 33)$
Robert Fraser Gallery, London

192 Cafe, Monte Carlo 1957
Pencil on paper, $6\frac{3}{4} \times 4\frac{3}{4}(17.2 \times 12)$
Private collection

193 Circo Togni 1957
Ink and crayon on paper
$8 \times 5\frac{3}{8}(20.3 \times 13.7)$
Waddington Galleries

Inscribed by the clown 'dal oglio lodovico'.

194 Girl reading 1957
Pencil on paper, $5\frac{3}{8} \times 8\frac{1}{4}(13.6 \times 21)$
Robert Fraser Gallery, London

195 Jake's Flowers 1960
Pencil on paper, $10 \times 9(25.3 \times 22.8)$
Private collection

195

Jake, young son of Joe and Jos Tilson, collected this bunch of flowers and grass while Blake was staying with the Tilsons on holiday at Nancledra in Cornwall where they had a cottage. Blake went there, 1959 and 1960.

196 Joe reading 1960
Pencil on paper
$11\frac{1}{2} \times 9(29.2 \times 22.8)$
Robert Fraser Gallery, London

Drawn in Cornwall, see Cat. no. 195.

197 Pram at St Ives 1960
Pen and ink on paper
$7\frac{1}{8} \times 4\frac{3}{8}(18.1 \times 11.1)$
Robert Fraser Gallery, London

Drawn on the same visit as Cat. no. 195.

198 Eric's Window 1961
Pencil on paper
$8 \times 5\frac{1}{4}(20.3 \times 13.3)$
Robert Fraser Gallery, London

Eric Gibson was a student at St. Martin's School of Art.

199 Pepper pot 1961
Pencil on paper
$5\frac{1}{2} \times 3\frac{5}{8}$(14 × 9.2)
Robert Fraser Gallery, London

A cardboard pepper pot drawn in the flat of Derek Boshier, a painter and friend of the artist.

200 Wrestling, Albert Hall 1961
Pencil on paper
$7\frac{1}{2} \times 4\frac{3}{4}$(19 × 12.1)
Waddington Galleries

201 Lime Grove Baths 1961
Pencil, 11 × 18(28 × 45.7)
Agnes and Frits Becht, Naarden, Holland

202 April, with Pipalo and Star King 1963
Pencil and white ink
20 × $25\frac{3}{4}$(50.8 × 65.4)
The Baltimore Museum of Art: Thomas E. Benesch Memorial Collection (BMA 1964. 116)

Pipalo and Star King were imaginary childhood companions of April Wilson, Blake's half-sister-in-law.

203 Bertram Mills Funfair Entrance 1967
Pencil and coloured pencils on paper, $12\frac{1}{2} \times 10$(31.7 × 25.4)
Private collection (London)

This and the following two drawings belong to a series of circus or funfair drawings executed during the Bertram Mills season at Olympia 1966–67. An earlier series is dated 1961.

204 Horses and Stalls 1967
Pencil and coloured pencils on paper
$12\frac{1}{2} \times 10$(31.8 × 25.4)
Private collection (London)

202

205 Botton Bros Bumper Cars II 1967
Pencil and coloured pencils on paper
$12\frac{1}{2} \times 10$(31.8 × 25.4)
Private collection (London)

206 Drawing for a Glamour Calendar 1968
Pencil and white ink on brown tinted paper
$25\frac{1}{2} \times 19\frac{1}{2}$(64.8 × 49.5)
Waddington Galleries

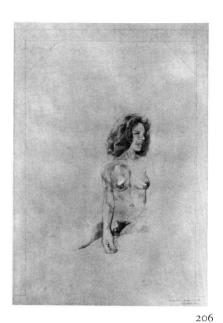

206

211

210 Mandy 1972
Pencil on paper
$22\frac{7}{8} \times 17\frac{3}{4}(58.1 \times 45.1)$
Erik and Lilott Berganus

A girl at Wellow.

211 Death of a Moth 1972
Pencil
$22\frac{3}{4} \times 18(57.7 \times 45.7)$
Peter Blake

A fairy drawing related to Blake's
Midsummer Night's Dream paintings
and watercolours but on an invented
theme. The gallery owner Anthony
D'Offay had a loose picture label 'Death
of a Butterfly' for which Blake made a
watercolour and he went on to do
'Death of a Moth'.

**207 Study for Tarzan (Boy, Jane
and Cheeta)** c.1968?
Pencil
$39\frac{3}{4} \times 30(101 \times 76.2)$
Giorgio Soavi, Milan

Related to cat. nos 150 and 151.

**208 A Mad Tea Party at Watts
Tower** c.1971
Pencil on paper
$25 \times 19\frac{1}{4}(63.5 \times 48.9)$
Klaus and Gertrude Anschel

Related to the painting (Cat. no. 103)
but started later.

209

209 Roses 1969
Pen and ink on paper
$22\frac{3}{4} \times 18(57.8 \times 45.7)$
Patrick Caulfield

Inscribed to Pat and Pauline Caulfield.
The stylisation of the outline mimics
that of Caulfield's own drawings.

FIVE NATURE AND
CULTURE DRAWINGS

**212 Plate 69. Czech Woman.
Photo by Professor Heinrich
Maass, Berlin** 1973–7
Pencil drawing
$23 \times 18(58.4 \times 45.7)$
Waddington Galleries

This drawing and the four following
were drawn in 7H pencil from a group
of 120 photographs published as a vol-
ume, 'Nature and Culture' selected by
Dr Peter Landow, 1928. The nudes are
all designated by country.

**213 Plate 84. Italian Woman.
Photo by E. O. Hoppé,
London** 1973–7
Pencil drawing
$23 \times 18(58.4 \times 45.7)$
Waddington Galleries

In the exhibition this will be displayed vertically 212

216

213

214

215

214 Plate 91. Bedouin Woman from Southern Tunis. Photo by Lehnert and Landrock, Cairo 1973–7
Pencil drawing
23 × 18(58.4 × 45.7)
Waddington Galleries

215 Plate 106. Javanese Woman. Photo by Medical Investigation Committee, Batavia. Lent by the Berlin Anthropological Society 1973–7
Pencil drawing
23 × 18(58.4 × 45.7)
Waddington Galleries

216 Plate 113. Girl from the Island of Bali. Photo by Dr Krause, Bali. Lent by Dr Karl With, Cologne (Property of the Publishing House Georg Müller, Munich) 1973–7
Pencil drawing
23 × 18(58.4 × 45.7)
Waddington Galleries

217

217 Fun Fair, Bath 1975
Pen and ink
11 × 8(28 × 20.5)
Private collection

218 Vase of Flowers 1975–7
Pencil on paper
23 × 17⅞(58.4 × 45.4)
Private collection

Drawn at Wellow.

219 Illustration p.2. Summer with Monica 1978
Pencil on paper
6 × 4½(15.2 × 11.5)
Waddington Galleries

Published by the Gee Whizzard Press in 'Summer with Monica', a long poem by Roger McGough (first edition 1967) for which Blake designed a cover and five illustrations in a variety of styles related to the changing moods of the poem.

ART WORK

220 Food 1957
Watercolour and gouache
3¾ × 15¾(9.5 × 40)
Peter Blake

As Blake was unable to sell his paintings at that time, he had to take on commercial work, so he accepted a commission from the Fatstock Marketing Corporation for the cover of a cookery book. The drawing was made from a 35 mm colour transparency held up to the light and took five weeks to complete, but in the event the transparency, not the drawing, was used.

221 Outside Grauman's Chinese Theatre 1963
Pencil and bodycolour
13 × 10(33 × 25.4)
Waddington Galleries

This and the next two drawings are part of a set of Hollywood and the neighbourhood made on a visit to Los Angeles in the winter of 1963 for *The Sunday Times* and published on 15 November 1964. Grauman's is a famous Hollywood tourist attraction. Film stars are invited to set their prints in concrete in front of it.

220

221

222 Mable Stark, an 80 year old Lion Tamer at Los Angeles 1963
Gouache and coloured pencil
$10\frac{3}{4} \times 8 (27.3 \times 20.3)$
Cecil Higgins Art Gallery, Bedford

Mabel Stark kept the Circus World Zoo where animal film-stars were exhibited. Blake met her but this drawing was made from a postcard.

223 Big Do-Nut Drive In 1963
Coloured pencils
$12 \times 10 (30.5 \times 25.4)$
Private collection

Drawn on 'location' in the San Fernando Valley, California.

224 Jean Harlow 1964
Cryla on hardboard
$17\frac{1}{2} \times 14\frac{1}{2} (44.5 \times 36.8)$
Mr and Mrs Terry Blake

Cover of *The Sunday Times Magazine*, 22 November 1964. Derived from a black and white photograph reproduced in the Hamburg catalogue, 1974, p.50. The signature is added from another photo. As in the contemporary 'Beatles' and 'Bo Diddley', there is a passage representing faulty registration in printing (at the top of the black area left) but here it comprises red, yellow and blue.

225 The Explosionist 1966
Oil and collage
$12\frac{5}{8} \times 9\frac{7}{8} (32 \times 25)$
Robert Shuman

This is an illustration to a story in a 'girlie' magazine. The idea is that all kinds of nasty things are in the box.

226 Marlene Dietrich 1967
Life-size cut-out
$69\frac{3}{4} \times 18 (177.2 \times 45.7)$
Private collection

One of a great number of figures collaged on to hardboard and used as a background to the Beatles for the sleeve of 'Sergeant Pepper's Lonely Hearts Club Band'. The idea for this cover was evolved by Blake and Jann Haworth in collaboration with the Beatles.

A sleeve had already been designed but Robert Fraser persuaded the Beatles that they should ask a painter to do it and Blake was chosen. The Beatles had had uniforms made and had worked out the idea that they should appear as

224

Sgt. Pepper's band. It was Blake's notion that the audience should be composed of cut-outs of famous people and names were chosen by the group, Robert Fraser and Blake. The format is very like that of the collages made by Blake in about 1957 (Cat. nos 109–111).

Waxworks of the group were borrowed from Mme Tussauds. The bust on the ground lower right was a favourite object of one of the group and was used as a model for Sergeant Pepper.

227 Portrait of Mary Wilson 1968
Cryla on hardboard
$7\frac{3}{4} \times 6(19.7 \times 15.3)$
Mrs Neville Burston

Cover of *The Sunday Times Magazine* 19 May 1968. Mary Wilson became a celebrity when her poems were published.

228 Miss Pears 1969
Cryla on canvas
$44\frac{1}{8} \times 34\frac{1}{4}(112 \times 87)$
A & F Pears Ltd, London

Miss Pears is selected from photographs sent in which are judged by a jury of which Blake was a member that year. He painted the winner from a photograph and crowned her Miss Pears. Pears had used Millais' 'Bubbles' as an advertisement for a long time.

229a Study for Royal Academy Summer Exhibition Poster 1975
Ink, coloured pencil and montage
$6\frac{1}{2} \times 6\frac{1}{4}(16.5 \times 15.8)$
Gordon and Jo House

Commissioned for the 207th Summer Exhibition 1975. This study does not resemble closely the finished poster which includes parts of several of Blake's own works, for example 'Liberty in a Kimono' (Cat. no. 161) and part of the abstract section of 'Got a Girl' (Cat. no. 47).

229a

229b Academy 1975
Collage
$17\frac{3}{4} \times 17\frac{3}{4}(45 \times 45)$
Galerie Meyer-Ellinger, Frankfurt

The artwork for the Academy poster.

230 Funny Way to be a Hero 1976
Collage
$11\frac{5}{8} \times 7\frac{3}{4}(29.5 \times 19.7)$
Leslie Waddington

Made as artwork for the cover of the book of the same name by John Fisher. It is a history of the music hall. Blake's design takes up again his collage style of the late 50s.

231 Gershwin's American in Paris
Oil on canvas
$20 \times 18(50.8 \times 45.7)$
Harveys of Bristol

Commissioned by Harveys. Although Gene Kelly was the star of the film 'An American in Paris' this head is a disguised Montgomery Clift.

231

Commissioned by Daimler as one of a series by artists and designers. The idea was that lucky purchasers of Daimlers would get a reproduction of the pictures or objects when buying selected cars.

234 Kenney Jones 1981
Oil on board
$5\frac{3}{4} \times 5\frac{3}{4}(14.6 \times 14.6)$
Waddington Galleries

Peter Blake was commissioned to do the sleeve for an album by The Who which was eventually called 'Face Dances'. Before the title was finally chosen from several, Blake had asked the fifteen best figurative painters he knew to make portraits of the members of the group from commissioned photographs. These were: Pete Townshend: Bill Jacklin, Tom Phillips, Colin Self, Richard Hamilton; Roger Daltrey: Michael Andrews, Alan Jones, David Inshaw, David Hockney; John Entwistle: Clive Barker, Ronald Kitaj, Howard Hodgkin, Patrick Caulfield; Kenney Jones: Peter Blake, Joe Tilson, Patrick Proctor, David Tindle. The portraits were printed as a poster that was inserted into the first run of the album and as a signed print given to disk jockeys and journalists.

232 Othello 1979
Watercolour
$9\frac{1}{8} \times 7\frac{1}{4}(22.9 \times 18.4)$
Waddington Galleries

The subject is Iago whispering to Othello. A set of paperback covers was commissioned from the Ruralists by Methuen for their Arden Shakespeare edition of the plays. The other three, drawn by Blake were 'Timon of Athens' 'Anthony and Cleopatra' and 'Henry IV part 2'. The commission came after one of the publishers had seen the film on the Ruralists by John Read on BBC Television.

233 Daimler 1980
Oil on canvas
$25\frac{1}{8} \times 21\frac{5}{8}(64 \times 55)$
Jaguar Cars Ltd.

BIBLIOGRAPHY

Compiled by Beth Houghton and Krzysztof Cieszkowski

1. Statements and writings by, and interviews with, the artist

2. Books, sections in books and entries from public and private collection catalogues

3. One-man exhibitions

4. Group exhibitions

5. Periodical and newspaper articles

Sections 1, 3, 4 and 5 are arranged chronologically by date of publication.

Section 2 is arranged alphabetically by author.

Sections 3 and 4 are lists of exhibitions for which a catalogue has been published unless stated otherwise in the entry. The number of works given in brackets in the group exhibition section refers to works exhibited by Peter Blake.

All items have been seen by the compilers except those marked *.

1. Statements and writings by, and interviews with, the artist

Supermidget with Mini-man [cartoon-strip]. *Ark : the journal of the Royal College of Art*, no. 24 [Winter 1959], p. 44.

Only sixteen [cartoon-strip]. *Ark : the journal of the Royal College of Art*, no. 25, 1960, p. 29.

Mervyn Levy. Peter Blake, Pop art for admass, (The artist at work, 23) [mostly interview]. *Studio International*, Nov. 1963 (vol. 166, no. 847), pp. 184–9.

Barry Joyce. Peter Blake : Pop artist [mostly interview]. *Modus Vivendi* : [college magazine of South-West Essex Technical College and School of Art], 31 Oct. 1966 (vol. 1, no. 1), pp. 12–14.

Blake being slightly contrary, *in* catalogue of exhibition *Three painters : Peter Blake, Jim Dine and Richard Hamilton*, Birmingham, Midlands Art Centre (Nov. 1967–Jan. 1968).

[comments] *in* David Bailey & Peter Evans. *Goodbye baby & amen : a saraband for the Sixties*. London : Condé Nast, 1969. pp. 43–44.

[texts reprinted from previous publications] *in* catalogue of one-man exhibition, Bristol, City Art Gallery (Nov.–Dec. 1969).

[introduction] *in* catalogue of Bath, Festival Gallery, exhibition of works by Peter Blake and Jann Haworth (June–July 1974).

[introduction] *in* catalogue of *Peter Blake's selection exhibition*, Bath, Festival Gallery (June–July 1974).

[statement] *in* catalogue of exhibition *European painting in the Seventies : new work by sixteen artists*, Los Angeles, County Museum of Art (Sept.–Nov. 1975).

[statement] *in* catalogue of exhibition *Arte inglese oggi 1960–1976*, Milan, Palazzo Reale (Feb.–May 1976).

[introduction] *in* catalogue of Waddington Galleries one-man exhibition, *Peter Blake : 'Souvenirs and samples'* (Apr.–May 1977).

Open letter : [published in the article] Tisdall, Cork and Overy are framed in Hayward Annual Part Two. Peter Blake's open letter, hanging at the Arts Council Summer Show, shows the successful school of British artists on the defensive. *Guardian*, 20 July 1977, p. 10.

Peter Blake in retrospect : [interview with Mike von Joel]. *Art Line*, no. 2, Nov. 1982, pp. 5–7.

Emma Parsons. Peter Blake, interviewed. *Arts Review Year Book*, 1983, pp. 46–7.

2. Books, sections in books and entries from public and private collection catalogues

Alley, Ronald. *British painting since 1945*. London : Tate Gallery, 1966, pp. [12, 42].

Alloway, Lawrence. The development of British pop, *in* Lucy Lippard (Ed.) *Pop art*. London : Thames and Hudson, 1966. pp. 28, 50, 52.

Amaya, Mario. *Pop as art : a survey of the new super realism*. London : Studio Vista, 1965. pp. 108–110.

Bailey, David, & Peter Evans. *Goodbye baby & amen ; a saraband for the Sixties*. London : Condé Nast, 1969. pp. 42–44.

Compton, Michael. *Art since 1945*. Milton Keynes : Open University, 1976 (units 15/16 of A351 course). p. 49.

Compton, Michael. *Pop art*. London : Hamlyn, 1970. (Movements of modern art) p. 61.

Dienst, Rolf-Gunter. *Pop art*. Wiesbaden : Limes, 1965. pp. 55–6.

Finch, Christopher. *Image as language : aspects of British art 1950–1968*. Harmondsworth : Penguin, 1969. pp. 69–72.

Hackney, Stephen. Peter Blake : 'The Masked Zebra Kid', *in* Stephen Hackney (Ed.) *Completing the picture : materials and techniques of twenty-six paintings in the Tate Gallery*. London : Tate Gallery, 1982. pp. 104–7.

Kultermann, Udo. *The new painting*. London : Pall Mall Press, 1969. p. 173.

Lucie-Smith, Edward. *Art today : from abstract expressionism to superrealism*. Oxford : Phaidon, 1977. pp. 250–1, 485. Originally published in Italian by Arnoldo Mondadori, Milan, 1976.

Lucie-Smith, Edward. *Movements in art since 1945*. Rev. ed. London: Thames and Hudson, 1975.

Melville, Robert. *Figurative art since 1945*. London: Thames and Hudson, 1971. pp.199–200.

Peter Stuyvesant Foundation. *Peter Stuyvesant Foundation: a collection in the making – 1965 purchases*; introd. by Michael Kaye and Alan Bowness. London: Peter Stuyvesant Foundation, 1965.

Pierre, José. *Pop art: an illustrated dictionary*. London: Eyre Methuen, 1977. pp.30–31. Translation of French ed. 1975.

Robertson, Bryan, John Russell and Lord Snowdon. *Private view*. London: Nelson, 1965. pp.224–7. Text by Robertson.

Russell, John, and Suzi Gablik. *Pop art redefined*. London: Thames and Hudson, 1969. p.40.

Sammlung Ludwig im Wallraf-Richartz Museum. *Kunst der sechziger Jahre: Sammlung Ludwig im Wallraf-Richartz Museum, Köln*; introd. by Gert von der Osten, Peter Ludwig, [et al.]. 4. verbesserte Auflage. Cologne: Wallraf-Richartz Museum, 1970.

Shone, Richard. *The century of change: British painting since 1900*. Oxford: Phaidon, 1977, pp.40, 210–1.

Tate Gallery. *Guide to the collections of the Tate Gallery*. London: Tate Gallery, 1970. p.43 (on Peter Blake's 'On the balcony' and 'Shop window').

Tate Gallery. *The Tate Gallery 1968–70* [biennial report]. London: Tate Gallery, 1970. pp.72–4 (on Peter Blake's 'The fine art bit' and 'Toy shop').

Tate Gallery. *The Tate Gallery, an illustrated companion to the national collections of British & modern foreign art*. London: Tate Gallery, 1979. p.134.

Tate Gallery. *The Tate Gallery 1978–80, illustrated biennial report*. London: Tate Gallery, 1980. pp.41–2 (on Peter Blake's 'Self-portrait with badges').

Tate Gallery. *The Tate Gallery 1978–80, illustrated catalogue of acquisitions*. London: Tate Gallery, 1981, pp.66–8 (on Peter Blake's 'Self-portrait with badges').

Tono, Yoshiaki (Ed.). *The pop image of man*. Tokyo: Kodansha, 1971, (Art Now, 4). p.82. Japanese text.

Usherwood, Nicholas. *The Brotherhood of Ruralists*. London: Lund Humphries, 1981.

Wilson, Simon. *Pop*. London: Thames and Hudson, 1974. pp.41–44.

3. One-man exhibitions

1960

*[Apr.?] London, Architectural Association. [Small private exhibition of Peter Blake's paintings on the occasion of the Presidential Reception]. [no catalogue traced].

1962

*Oct. London, Portal Gallery. Peter Blake. [no catalogue traced].

1965

Oct.–Nov. London, Robert Fraser Gallery. *Peter Blake*. (23 works). Catalogue notes by Robert Melville.

1969

July. London, Leslie Waddington Prints. *Peter Blake: French postcards, exhibition of screenprints*. [no catalogue traced – private view card].

July–Sept. London, Robert Fraser Gallery. *Peter Blake: drawings, watercolours and art work originals 1968–9*. (38 works).

Nov.–Dec. Bristol, City Art Gallery. *Peter Blake*. (149 works). Introd. by Roger Coleman; includes texts reprinted from earlier publications, by Robert Melville, Peter Blake, etc.

1970

Sept.–Oct. Farnham, Ashgate Gallery. *10th anniversary exhibition: Peter Blake*. (16 works).

1972

Dec. London, Waddington Galleries I. *Peter Blake: watercolours and drawings*. (no list of works; 5 works illustrated).

1973

Sept.–Nov. Amsterdam, Stedelijk Museum. *Peter Blake*. (55 works). Travelling to Hamburg, Brussels and Arnhem. Introd. by Rainer Crone.

Dec.–Jan. 1974. Hamburg, Kunstverein in Hamburg. *Peter Blake*. (81 works). Travelling to Brussels and Arnhem. Introd. by Uwe M. Schneede.

1974

Feb.–Mar. Brussels, Palais des Beaux-Arts. *Peter Blake*. (55 works). Travelling to Arnhem. Introd. by Rainer Crone.

*Apr.–May. London, Natalie Stern. [*Peter Blake: print retrospective*]. [no catalogue traced].

1977

Apr.–May. London, Waddington and Tooth Galleries I. *Peter Blake: Souvenirs and samples*. (142 works). Introd. by Peter Blake.

1978

London, Waddington Graphics. *Peter Blake: 'Side-show' 1974–78: Fat boy, Bearded lady, Tattooed man, Giant, Midget. Five wood engravings 1978*.

1979

Mar.–Apr. Henley-on-Thames, Bohun Gallery. *Peter Blake: drawings and prints*. (22 works).

1983

Feb.–Mar. London, Tate Gallery. *Peter Blake*. (234 works). Introd. by Michael Compton, Nicholas Usherwood and Robert Melville.

4. Group exhibitions

1954

May–Aug. London, Royal Academy of Arts. *Summer exhibition*. (1 work).

1955

*Exeter. [*Paintings by tutors and students of the Royal College of Art*]. [no catalogue traced].

*London, R.W.S. Galleries. [*The Observer exhibition of portraits of children*]. (2 works). [no catalogue traced].

Apr.–May. London, New Burlington Galleries. *Daily Express young artists' competition.* (1 work).

Apr.–Aug. London, Royal Academy of Arts. *Summer exhibition.* (1 work).

1956

*July–Aug. London, Prospect Gallery. [*Summer selection : annual mixed show*]. [no catalogue traced].

1958

Jan.–Feb. London, Institute of Contemporary Arts. *Five painters* [John Barnicoat, Peter Blake, Peter Corviello, William Green, Richard Smith]. (11 works). Introd. by Roger Coleman.

May–June. London, Whitechapel Art Gallery. *The Guggenheim painting award 1958 : British section.* (1 work).

1959

*Cambridge. [*Six from now*]. [no catalogue traced].

1960

London, Institute of Contemporary Arts. *Theo Crosby : sculpture ; Peter Blake : objects ; John Latham : libraries.* (13 works). Introd. by Lawrence Alloway.

Jan.–Feb. London, New Vision Centre Gallery. *Grass, by Tony Gifford, and Gold, by Peter Blake.* (12 works).

Mar.–Apr. London, Portal Gallery. *Peter Blake, Roddy Maude-Roxby, Ivor Abrahams.* (25 works).

Oct.–Dec. London, Institute of Contemporary Arts. *The mysterious sign.* (1 work). Introd. by Robert Melville.

*Nov. London, Portal Gallery [*DANAD design*]. [no catalogue traced].

1961

*London, R.B.A. Galleries. [*The young Commonwealth artists exhibition*]. (2 works). [no catalogue traced].

*London, Raille Gallery. [*Momentum*]. [no catalogue traced].

Feb.–Mar. London, Brook Street Gallery. *Aspects of collage.* (2 works).

Oct. London, Rawinsky Gallery. *6 painters, 2 sculptors : an exhibition of drawings.* (4 works). Introd. by Jasia Reichardt.

Nov.–Dec. London, A.I.A. Gallery. *Peter Blake, Pauline Boty, Geoffrey Reeve, Christine Porter.* (6 works).

Nov.–Jan. 1962. Liverpool, Walker Art Gallery. *The John Moores' Liverpool exhibition 1961.* (1 work).

1962

*Oslo. [*Modern British paintings*]. [no catalogue traced].

Mar.–Apr. London, Institute of Contemporary Arts. *Prizewinners of the John Moores' Liverpool exhibition 1961.* (1 work).

Feb.–Sept. London, Arts Council of Great Britain. *British self-portraits from Sickert to the present day.* (1 work). Opening in Newcastle upon Tyne, Laing Art Gallery ; travelling to Leeds, Birmingham, Aberystwyth, Leicester, Salford, Guildford and Bournemouth. Introd. by Lawrence Gowing.

Apr. London, Arthur Tooth & Sons. *British painting and sculpture today and yesterday.* (4 works).

Summer. London. A.I.A. Gallery. *Summer 1962 : a selection of paintings by members of the A.I.A.* (1 work).

*June. London, Congress House. [*Festival of labour : exhibition of new art*]. [no catalogue traced].

Aug.–Sept. London, Arthur Jeffress Gallery. *New approaches to the figure.* (2 works).

Oct. Cheltenham, Art Gallery. *Six young painters : Peter Blake, William Crozier, John Hoyland, Sonia Lawson, Dorothy Mead, Euan Uglow.* (6 works).

Nov.–Dec. London, Royal College of Art. '*Towards art?' : an exhibition showing the contribution which the College has made to the Fine Arts 1952–1962.* (3 works).

*Nov.–Dec. New York, Sidney Janis Gallery. *New realists.* (1 work).

Nov.–Dec. San Francisco, Museum of Art. *British art today.* (2 works). Travelling to Dallas and Santa Barbara. Introd. by Lawrence Alloway.

1963

Jan.–Feb. London, Arthur Tooth & Sons. *1962 : one year of British art selected by Edward Lucie-Smith.* (4 works).

Feb.–Mar. London, Grabowski Gallery. *Exhibition of drawings by artists of two generations.* (5 works). Introd. by Bryan Robertson.

May–June. Nottingham, Midland Group. *Pop art.* (4 works).

May–Oct. London, Arts Council of Great Britain. *Towards art?* [touring exhibition selected from Royal College of Art exhibition (Nov.–Dec. 1962), commencing in Cambridge]. (2 works). Introd. by Carel Weight.

June. London, Whitechapel Art Gallery and Tate Gallery. *British painting in the Sixties.* (3 works). Exhibition organised by Contemporary Art Society.

June–July. London, Robert Fraser Gallery. *Obsession and fantasy.* (2 works).

Aug.–Sept. Zürich, Helmhaus. *Englische Malerei der Gegenwart.* (1 work). Introd. by Alan Bowness. Organised by Contemporary Art Society, based on exhibition at Whitechapel Art Gallery and Tate Gallery (June 1963).

Sept.–Oct. Fredericton (New Brunswick), Beaverbrook Art Gallery. *The Dunn International : an exhibition of contemporary painting.* (1 work). Travelling to London, Tate Gallery. Foreword by M. Beaverbrook.

Sept.–Nov. Paris, Musée d'Art Moderne de la Ville de Paris. *Biennale de Paris (Troisième).* (19 works). British section introd. by Norbert Lynton.

Nov.–Dec. London, Tate Gallery. *Dunn International : an exhibition of contemporary painting sponsored by the Sir James Dunn Foundation.* (1 work). Organised by the Arts Council of Great Britain.

Dec. London, Robert Fraser Gallery. [*Drawings, gouaches and collages*]. (19 works).

1964

Belfast, Arts Council of Northern Ireland. *The new image.* (2 works). Introd. by Ronald Alley.

*Düsseldorf, Kunstverein für die Rheinlande und Westfalen. [*Britische Malerei der Gegenwart*]. [no catalogue traced].

*Ghent, Museum voor Schone Kunsten. [*Figuratie en Defiguratie*]. [no catalogue traced].

London, Arts Council of Great Britain. *6 young painters : Peter Blake, William Crozier, David Hockney, Dorothy Mead, Bridget Riley, Euan Uglow.* (5 works).

London, Arts Council of Great Britain. *New painting 61–64.* (1 work). Introd. by Ronald Alley.

*Jan. London, Royal College of Art. [*British painting from the Paris Biennale 1963*]. [no catalogue traced].

Apr. Stratford-upon-Avon. *Shakespeare exhibition, 1564–1964.* (3 works). Travelling to Edinburgh and London. Introd. by Richard Buckle, etc.

Apr.–June. Bochum, Städtische Kunstgalerie. *Profile III : Englische Kunst der Gegenwart.* (3 works). Introd. by Sir Herbert Read, Roland Penrose.

Apr.–June. London, Tate Gallery. *Painting & sculpture of a decade : 54–64.* (3 works). Organised by the Calouste Gulbenkian Foundation.

June–Aug. Hague, Haags Gemeentemuseum. *Nieuwe realisten.* (2 works). Text by L.J.F. Wijsenbeek, Jasia Reichardt, Pierre Restany.

Summer. London, Robert Fraser Gallery. *Summer exhibition 1964.* (9 works).

Oct.–Jan. 1965. Pittsburgh, Carnegie Institute, Museum of Art. *The 1964 Pittsburgh International.* (1 work).

Nov. London, Institute of Contemporary Arts. *I.C.A. screen-print project.* [Prints produced by Kelpra Studio]. (1 work).

Nov.–Dec. Cardiff, National Museum of Wales. *Pick of the pops.* (3 works). Introd. by John Ingamells.

Nov.–Jan. 1965. Berlin, Akademie der Künste. *Neue Realisten & Pop Art.* (2 works). Introd. by Werner Hofmann.

1965

London, Café Royal. *Café Royal centenary exhibition, 1865–1965.* (1 work). Introd. by Sir John Rothenstein.

London, Whitechapel Art Gallery. *Peter Stuyvesant Foundation : a collection in the making – 1965 purchases.* (1 work). Introd. by Michael Kaye.

*Feb.–Mar. Brussels, Palais des Beaux-Arts. *Pop art, nouveau idéalisme.* [no catalogue traced].

Feb.–Mar. Minneapolis, Walker Art Center. *London : the new scene.* (8 works). Travelling to Washington, Boston, Seattle, Vancouver, Toronto and Ottawa. Organised by Calouste Gulbenkian Foundation and British Council. Introd. by Martin Friedman, Alan Bowness.

May–Aug. London, Royal Academy of Arts. *Summer exhibition.* (3 works).

June–July. Oxford, Bear Lane Gallery. *Trends in contemporary British painting.* (1 work). Introd. by Ronald Alley.

July–Sept. London, Robert Fraser Gallery. [Group show]. (7 works).

*Oct. Paris, Galerie Creuze. *La figuration narrative dans l'art contemporain.*

*Oct.–Nov. Toronto, Art Gallery of Toronto. [*Focus on drawings : Canada/Great Britain/Italy/Spain*].

Nov.–Dec. New York, Marlborough-Gerson Gallery. *The English eye.* (1 work). Introd. by Robert Melville, Bryan Robertson.

1966

Feb.–Mar. New York, Solomon R. Guggenheim Museum. *European drawings.* (4 works). Introd. by Lawrence Alloway.

*Mar.–Apr. London, Robert Fraser Gallery. [*Work in progress*]. [no catalogue traced].

June. Milan, Studio Marconi. *Peter Blake, Derek Boshier, Patrick Caulfield, Richard Hamilton, Eduardo Paolozzi.* (5 works). Introd. by Christopher Finch.

Aug.–Sept. Dublin, National College of Art, Gallery. *Irish exhibition of living art.* (1 work).

Dec.–Mar. 1967. London, Ely House, Oxford University Press. *How they started : paintings by some former students of the Royal College of Art.* (1 work).

1967

*New York, Museum of Modern Art. *British drawings, the new generation : 57 works on paper by 18 artists.* Touring exhibition. [no catalogue traced].

Jan. London, Robert Fraser Gallery. *Works from 1956 to 1967 by Clive Barker, Peter Blake, Richard Hamilton, Jann Haworth and Colin Self.*

June–Sept. Geneva, Musée Rath. *Le visage de l'homme dans l'art contemporain.* (1 work). Introd. by M. Pianzola and C. Goerg.

Summer. London, Robert Fraser Gallery. *Summer exhibition 1967.* (1 work).

*July. London, Robert Fraser Gallery. [*Tribute to Robert Fraser*]. [no catalogue traced].

Oct. Brussels, Palais des Beaux-Arts. *Jeunes peintres anglais = Jonge Britse schilders.* (6 works). Introd. by Richard Morphet.

Oct.–Dec. Zürich, Galerie Bischofberger. *Englische Kunst.* (6 works in 2nd part of exhibition, Nov.–Dec. 1967).

Oct.–Jan. 1968. Pittsburgh, Carnegie Institute, Museum of Art. *1967 Pittsburgh International exhibition of contemporary painting and sculpture.* (1 work). Introd. by Gustave von Groschwitz.

Nov.–Dec. London, Royal College of Art Galleries. *Convocation exhibition : some paintings and drawings from the Royal College of Art collection.* (2 works).

Nov.–Dec. London, Tate Gallery. *Recent British painting : Peter Stuyvesant Collection.* (2 works). Introd. by Alan Bowness.

Nov.–Jan. 1968. Birmingham, Midlands Art Centre. *Three painters : Peter Blake, Jim Dine and Richard Hamilton.* (6 works). Travelling to Cambridge. Introd. by Robert Melville, Peter Cox, Peter Blake.

Dec. New York, Sidney Janis Gallery. *Homage to Marilyn Monroe.* (1 work).

1968

*Amsterdam, Galerie 20. [*Peter Blake, Jann Haworth : Holland homage*]. [no catalogue traced].

London, Arts Council of Great Britain. *Painting 64–67.* (1 work). Touring exhibition. Introd. by John Russell.

*London, Ely House, Oxford University Press. [*Old Testament drawings*]. [no catalogue traced].

Mar.–May. Hamburg, Kunstverein in Hamburg. *Britische Kunst heute.* (3 works). Introd. by Hans Platte.

Apr.–May. Eindhoven, Stedelijk van Abbemuseum. *'Three blind mice'/de collecties : Visser, Peeters, Becht.* (1 work). Introd. by W.A.L. Beeren.

Apr.–May. London, Institute of Contemporary Arts. *The obsessive image, 1960–1968.* (2 works). Introd. by Roland Penrose, Robert Melville, Mario Amaya.

Apr.–May. London, Robert Fraser Gallery. *Group show.* (6 works).

Apr.–June. Saint-Paul, Fondation Maeght. *L'art vivant, 1965–1968.* (2 works). Introd. by F. Wehrlin.

May–Aug. London, Royal Academy of Arts. *Summer exhibition.* (1 work).

June. Oxford, Bear Lane Gallery. *From Kitaj to Blake : non-abstract artists in Britain.* (2 works).

Sept.–Nov. Darmstadt, Kunsthalle. *Menschenbilder : Ausstellung zum 10. Darmstädter Gesprach.* (2 works). Introd. by Arnold Gehlen, etc.

1969

July–Sept. London, Arts Council of Great Britain (in Hayward Gallery). *Pop art.* (3 works). Introd. by John Russell, Suzi Gablik.

Nov.–Jan. 1970. Liverpool, Walker Art Gallery. *7th John Moores' Liverpool exhibition.* (1 work).

1970

Mar.–Apr. London, Waddington Galleries I. *Works on paper.* (1 work).

May–July. London, Royal Academy of Arts. *Summer exhibition.* (1 work).

May–July. Recklinghausen, Städtische Kunsthalle. *Zeitgenossen : das Gesicht unserer Gesellschaft im Spiegel der heutigen Kunst (Ruhrfestspiele Recklinghausen).* (1 work). Introd. by H.L.C. Jaffé.

June–July. London, Arts Council of Great Britain (in Hayward Gallery). *Kelpra prints.* (1 work). Introd. by Ronald Alley, Joe Tilson.

June–Sept. Knokke-het Zoute, Gemeentelijk Casino. *Pop art : nieuwe figuratie = nouveau réalisme.* (3 works). Introd. by John Russell, Pierre Restany.

Aug.–Nov. Darmstadt, Mathildenhöhe. *3. Internationale der Zeichnung.* (3 works). Texts by H. Knell, I. Pan.

Sept.–Oct. Tokyo, National Museum of Modern Art. *Contemporary British art.* (1 work). Introd. by Andrew Causey.

Nov.–Jan. 1971. London, Arts Council of Great Britian (at Whitechapel Art Gallery). *3 → ∞ : new multiple art.* (1 work by Peter Blake and Jann Haworth). Introd. by Janet Daley, Karl Gerstner.

Nov.–Jan. 1971. London, Mayfair Gallery. *Pop! '70.* (3 works). Introd. by Ira D. Gale.

Nov.–Jan. 1971. Washington, National Gallery of Art. *British painting and sculpture 1960–1970 : an exhibition organised by the Tate Gallery and the British Council.* (5 works). Introd. by Edward Lucie-Smith.

Dec. London, Waddington Galleries. *Alice : an exhibition of paintings, drawings and screenprints by Peter Blake and Graham Ovenden based on the theme of Lewis Carroll's 'Alice'.*

1971

*London, Mayfair Gallery. [Group exhibition]. [no catalogue traced].

*Jan. London, Angela Flowers. *Post card show.* [no catalogue traced].

Feb.–Mar. London, Waddington Galleries I. *Works on paper.* (1 work).

Mar. London, Arthur Tooth & Sons. *Critics choice : 1971 selection by Robert Melville.* (2 works).

Apr.–June. Brussels, Palais des Beaux-Arts. *Métamorphose de l'object : art et anti-art, 1910–1970.* (1 work). Introd. by Werner Haftmann, etc.

1972

Nov.–Dec. London, Angela Flowers. *British drawings 1952–1972.* (1 work).

1973

*Oxford, Bear Lane Gallery. [*Spring collection*]. [no catalogue traced].

*Paris, Galerie Stadler. [*Estampes anglaises actuelles*]. [no catalogue traced].

May–June. Baden–Baden, Kunsthalle. *11 Englische Zeichner.* (23 works). Travelling to Bremen. Organised by Gesellschaft der Freunde junger Kunst. Introd. by Timothy Hilton.

Aug.–Oct. Edinburgh, Scottish Arts Council (in Scottish National Gallery of Modern Art). *Earth images : an exhibition of ceramic sculpture.* (2 works).

Sept.–Nov. Brussels, Palais des Beaux–Arts. *Henry Moore to Gilbert & George : modern British art from the Tate Gallery.* (1 work). Organised by Tate Gallery and British Council. Introd. by Anne Seymour.

1974

June–July. Bath, Festival Gallery. *Peter Blake* [with works by Jann Haworth]. (54 works). Introd. by Peter Blake.

Aug.–Sept. Bath, Festival Gallery. *Peter Blake's selection exhibition.* (1 work). Introd. by Peter Blake.

Sept.–Nov. London, Arts Council of Great Britain (in Hayward Gallery). *British painting '74.* (2 works). Introd. by Andrew Forge.

Oct. London, Waddington Galleries I. *Works on paper.* (2 works).

1975

*Feb. London, Kinsman Morrison Gallery. [*British sculpture and objects*]. [no catalogue traced].

May–July. Darmstadt, Kunsthalle. *Realismus und Realität : Ausstellung zum 11. Darmstädter Gespräch.* (3 works). Introd. by H.W. Sabais, Bernd Krimmel.

*Aug.–Sept. Brisbane, Queensland National Art Gallery. *British artists' prints.* Introd. by Edward Lucie-Smith.

Sept.–Nov. Los Angeles, County Museum of Art. *European painting in the Seventies : new work by sixteen artists.* (5 works). Travelling to St. Louis and Madison (Wis.) Introd. by Maurice Tuchman, Peter Blake.

1976

Feb.–Mar. Hamburg, Kunstverein in Hamburg. *Pop art in England : Anfänge einer neuen Figuration 1947–63.* (4 works).

Travelling to Munich and York. Introd. by Uwe M. Schneede, Frank Whitford.

Feb.–May. Milan, Palazzo Reale. *Arte inglese oggi 1960–76*. (15 works). Organised by British Council. Introd. by Norbert Lynton.

May–July. Rotterdam, Museum Boymans-van Beuningen. *Peter Blake, Richard Hamilton, David Hockney, R.B. Kitaj, Eduardo Paolozzi*. (22 works). Introd. by Toni del Renzio.

May–July. York, York Art Gallery. *'Just what is it . . .?' : pop art in England*. (4 works). Organised by Arts Council of Great Britain. Introd. by Frank Whitford.

May–Aug. London, Royal Academy of Arts. *Summer exhibition*. (6 works).

1977

May–Sept. London, Arts Council of Great Britain (in Hayward Gallery). *1977 Hayward Annual : current British art, selected by Michael Compton, Howard Hodgkin and William Turnbull*. (4 works in Part 2, July–Sept. 1977).

June. Bath, Festival Gallery. *The Brotherhood of Ruralists*. (6 works). Travelling to Edinburgh, Doncaster and Southampton.

Sept.–Nov. London, Royal Academy of Arts. *British painting 1952–1977*. (2 works). Introd. by Frederick Gore.

1978

Apr. London, Waddington Galleries. *Groups*. (1 work).

May. Bodmin, Bodmin Fine Arts Gallery. *The Brotherhood of Ruralists*. (1 work). Introd. by Ian MacWatt.

May–Aug. London, Royal Academy of Arts. *Summer exhibition*. (5 works).

1979

Jan.–Feb. London, Waddington Galleries. *Groups II*. (1 work).

June–July. Seaford (Sussex), Charleston Manor. *The Brotherhood of Ruralists : paintings and drawings*. (10 works).

Aug.–Sept. Sudbury (Suffolk), Gainsborough's House. *The Brotherhood of Ruralists*. (5 works).

Nov.–Dec. Venice (Calif.), L.A. Louver Gallery. *This knot of life : an exhibition of current British painting and drawing presented in two parts*. (6 works). Introd. by Peter Goulds, R.B. Kitaj.

1980

Feb.–Mar. London, Waddington Galleries. *Groups III*. (1 work).

May–June. Brighton, Brighton Museum. *Fairies*. (2 works). Introd. by Alison Packer, Stella Beddoe, Lianne Jannett.

July–Aug. Bristol, City of Bristol Museum & Art Gallery. *Ophelia : paintings and drawings on the theme of Ophelia by the Brotherhood of Ruralists*. (1 work). Introd. by Arnold Wilson.

Oct.–Nov. Wellington, National Art Gallery. *Prints of the 70s by six British artists*. (15 works). Travelling to Wanganui, Auckland, Palmerston North, Christchurch and Dunedin. Organised by New Zealand Art Gallery Directors' Council. Introd. by Anne Kirker.

Dec.–Jan. 1981. London, Angela Flowers. *Nudes*. (2 works).

1981

Feb. London, Waddington Galleries. *Groups IV*. (3 works).

Apr.–May. Bristol, Arnolfini Gallery. *The Ruralists : an exhibition of works by the Brotherhood of Ruralists and their circle*. (11 works). Travelling to Birmingham, Glasgow and London (Camden Arts Centre). Introd. by Nicholas Usherwood.

June–July. London, Waddington Galleries. *Six British artists, prints 1974–81 : Peter Blake, Patrick Caulfield, Richard Hamilton, Allen Jones, Tom Phillips, Joe Tilson*. (21 works).

1982

Jan. London, Waddington Galleries. *Groups V*. (5 works).

Mar.–Apr. Peking, Art Gallery. *British drawings and watercolours*. (2 works). Travelling to Shenyang and Hong Kong. Organised by British Council. Introd. by John Gage, William Feaver.

May–Aug. London, Royal Academy of Arts. *Summer exhibition*. (6 works).

5. Periodical and newspaper articles

Neville Wallis. Designs for tomorrow: [including reference to 1956 Prospect Gallery exhibition]. *Observer*, 12 Aug. 1956 (no. 8615), p. 10.

R.C. [Roger Coleman]. A romantic naturalist : some notes on the paintings of Peter Blake. *Ark : the journal of the Royal College of Art*, no. 18, Nov. 1956, pp. 60–1.

Roger Coleman. The art of counterfeit. *The Painter & Sculptor : a journal of the visual arts*, 1958 (vol. 1, no. 1), pp. 21–3.

Robert Melville. [review of the 1958 I.C.A. exhibition], p. 278 *in* Exhibitions : paintings. *Architectural Review*, Apr. 1958 (vol. 123, no. 735), pp. 278–9.

Peter Blake. Supermidget with Mini-man [cartoon-strip]. *Ark : the journal of the Royal College of Art*, no. 24, [Winter 1959], p. 44.

Is it art? [review of 1960 I.C.A. group exhibition : Crosby, Blake, Latham]. *Daily Sketch*, 20 Jan. 1960, p. 4.

[Peter Blake]. Only sixteen [cartoon-strip]. *Ark : the journal of the Royal College of Art*, no. 25, 1960, p. 29.

Robert Melville. [review of March–April 1960 Portal Gallery group exhibition]. p. 424, *in* Exhibitions : painting and sculpture. *Architectural Review*, June 1960 (vol. 127, no. 760), pp. 422–4.

Peter Blake. Circus drawings [no text]. *The Painter & Sculptor : a journal of the visual arts*, Summer 1961 (vol. 4, no. 2), pp. 25–8.

*Eric Newton. The Moores' experiment. *Guardian*, 15 Nov. 1961.

Competition for adventurous artists : [review of 1961/62 John Moores' Liverpool exhibition]. *The Times*, 15 Nov. 1961, p. 19.

Robin Ironside. The prize paintings : [review of 1961/62 John Moores' Liverpool exhibition]. *Sunday Times*, 19 Nov. 1961, p. 38.

Jasia Reichardt. [review of 1961/62 John Moores' Liverpool exhibition], *in* Modern art in London. *Apollo*, Dec. 1961 (vol. 75, no. 442), pp. 199–200.

Philip Radcliffe. Art of success : Elvis gets in the show [on 1961/62 John Moores'

Liverpool exhibition]. *Daily Mail*, 11 Dec. 1961, p.10.

Keith Sutton. [review of 1961 A.I.A. group exhibition], *in* Round the London art galleries. *Listener*, 14 Dec. 1961, p.1038.

Blake's stake for stardom: [review of 1961 A.I.A. group exhibition]. *Topic*, 16 Dec. 1961, p.35.

Neville Wallis. [review of 1961 A.I.A. group exhibition]. *in* School of satire. *Observer*, 17 Dec. 1961, p.20.

Albert Hand. Elvis Monthly makes society. *Elvis Monthly*, 1962 (3rd. series, no.3), p.[14].

Dennis Farr. The John Moores' Liverpool Exhibition 3. *Burlington Magazine*, Jan. 1962 (vol.104, no.706), pp.30–1.

G.S. Whittet. The Liverpool biennial: [review of 1961/62 John Moores' Liverpool exhibition]. *Studio*, Feb. 1962 (vol.63, no.826), pp.70–1.

John Russell. Pioneer of Pop art (People of the 60's). *Sunday Times Colour Section*, 4 Feb. 1962, pp.16–17.

Keith Sutton. [reviews of 1962 Arthur Tooth, and I.C.A. group exhibitions] *in* Country from the heart. *Listener*, 12 Apr. 1962, p.647.

[reviews of 1962 Arthur Tooth and I.C.A. group exhibitions] *in* New steps to figuration. *Topic*, 14 Apr. 1962, p.10.

Anita Brookner. [review of 1962 Arthur Tooth exhibition], p.227 *in* Current and forthcoming exhibitions: London. *Burlington Magazine*, May 1962 (vol.104, no.710), pp.224–7.

G.S. Whittet. [review of 1962 Arthur Tooth group exhibition], p.233 *in* Figure in the frame. *Studio*, June 1962 (vol.163, no.830) pp.233–4.

Robert Melville. [review of 1962 Arthur Tooth group exhibition], pp.58–9 *in* Exhibitions: paintings and sculpture. *Architectural Review*, July 1962 (vol.132, no.785), pp.57–9.

How good is 'pop' art? – a topical question: humour and bravura in new British art. *The Illustrated London News*, 1 Sept. 1962, p.333.

John Russell. [review of 1962 Jeffress Gallery group exhibition] *in* Getting their message right. *Sunday Times*, 2 Sept. 1962, p.32.

John Russell. [review of 1962 Arthur Jeffress group exhibition] *in* Art news from London: Williams, Blake. *Art News*, Oct. 1962 (vol.61, no.6), p.49.

Mr Peter Blake: [review of 1962 Portal Gallery one-man exhibition] *in* Bedford Gallery's good showing. *The Times*, 27 Oct. 1962, p.4.

Jane Stockwood. Art: Peter Blake, Portal Gallery. *Queen*, 30 Oct. 1962 (vol.221, no.5499), p.20.

Edwin Mullins. Sculpture and mechanics. *Apollo*, Nov. 1962 (vol.76, no.9), pp.712–4.

Robert Melville. The durable expendables of Peter Blake. *Motif*, no.10, Winter 1962/3, pp.15–29.

Gerald Nordland. [review of 1962 San Francisco Museum of Art group exhibition, British art today], p.17, *in* Europe in California. *Arts Magazine*, May–June 1963 (vol.37, no.9), pp.16–18.

John Dalton. Midland Pop: [review of 1963 Nottingham, Midland Group group exhibition]. *Guardian*, 4 June 1963, p.7.

Robert Melville. [review of 1963 C.A.S. group exhibition, British painting in the Sixties], p.133, *in* Exhibitions: painting and sculpture. *Architectural Review*, Aug. 1963 (vol.134, no.798), pp.131–3.

Mervyn Levy. Peter Blake, pop art for admass, (The Artist at work, 23), [mostly interview]. *Studio International*, Nov. 1963 (vol.166, no.847), pp.184–9.

Robert Harvey. Pop. *Granta*: [magazine of Cambridge Students' Union], 30 Nov. 1963 (vol.68, no.1231), Modern art issue, pp.6–7.

Peter Blake: [article based on interview with Stuart Wright]. *Double Polygraph*: [college magazine of Chiswick Polytechnic], [no issue number or date, 1964?], pp.2–4.

Robert Melville. English Pop art. *Quadrum*, no.17, 1964, pp.23–38.

David Sylvester. Art in a cold climate. *Sunday Times Colour Magazine*, 25 Jan. 1964, pp.14–23.

Keith Roberts. [review of Blake's works in exhib. at RCA Galleries of British contributions to Paris Biennale 1963]. p.138 *in* Current and forthcoming exhibitions. *Burlington Magazine*, March 1964 (vol.106, no.732), pp.137–142.

Robert Melville. Fear of the banal [includes discussion of 'Self-portrait with badges']. *Architectural Review*, Apr. 1964 (vol.135, no.806), p.291.

J. Roger Baker. Everything's coming up Shakespeare: [on the planning for the Shakespeare exhibition, Stratford-upon-Avon, 1964]. *Tatler*, 15 Apr. 1964, pp.152–9.

Peter Blake in Hollywood: [6 drawings]. *Sunday Times Colour Magazine*, 15 Nov. 1964, pp.27–31.

Gérald Gassiot-Talabot. La figuration narrative dans la peinture contemporaine. *Quadrum*, no.18, 1965, pp.5–40.

Will Jones. Pop goes the artist: [review of 1965 Walker Art Center, Minneapolis group exhibition]. *Minneapolis Morning Tribune*, 5 Feb. 1965.

John K. Sherman. The new scene in London is a swinging one: [review of 1965 Walker Art Center, Minneapolis group exhibition]. *Minneapolis Sunday Tribune*, 14 Feb. 1965.

John Russell. London/NYC: the two-way traffic. *Art in America*, April 1965 (vol.53, no.2), pp.126–136. (pp.134, 6 on Blake).

[Michael Compton]. 'The Lettermen' by Peter Blake: [a new acquisition]. *Ferens Art Gallery, Kingston-upon-Hull, Bulletin*, April–June 1965, pp.[1–2].

Sidney Simon. From England's green and pleasant bowers: [review of 1965 Walker Art Center, Minneapolis group exhibition]. *Art News*, April 1965 (vol.64, no.2), pp.28–31, 64–65.

Pierre Jeannerat. Question raised by this and other exhibits at the R.A.: who's pulling whose leg? *Daily Mail*, 30 Apr. 1965, p.13.

*Frederick Laws. Royal Academy Summer Exhibition. *Guardian*, 30 Apr. 1965.

Making the Academy go pop: on the walls this year . . . a toy shop with real door, real window and real toys. *Sun*, 30 Apr. 1965, p.3.

Jasia Reichardt. La jeune génération en Grande Bretagne. *Aujourd'hui art et architecture*, July 1965 (no. 50), pp. 68–81.

John Russell. [review of 1965 Robert Fraser Gallery one-man exhibition] *in* Pro-American activities. *Sunday Times Weekly Review*, 25 July 1965, (no. 7419), p. 32.

Robert Melville. Pom-Pom: [review of 1965 Robert Fraser Gallery one-man exhibition]. *New Statesman*, 6 Aug. 1965, p. 196.

James Burr. [review of 1965 Robert Fraser Gallery one-man exhibition], p. 341 *in* The agonies of human protest. *Apollo*, Oct. 1965 (vol. 82, no. 44), pp. 340–2.

Robert Melville. Nice people: [review of 1965 Robert Fraser Gallery one-man exhibition]. *New Statesman*, 5 Nov. 1965, p. 707.

Bryan Robertson. Innocence and experience: Peter Blake and Brett Whiteley. *Spectator*, 5 Nov. 1965, p. 586.

John Russell. Peter Blake [review of 1965 Robert Fraser one-man exhibition], pp. 54–5 *in* Art news from London. *Art News*, Dec. 1965 (vol. 64, no. 8), pp. 36, 54–5.

J.R. [Joseph Rykwert]. Peter Blake alla Robert Fraser, *in* Mostre a Londra. *Domus*, Dec. 1965 (no. 433), p. 34.

G.S. Whittet. [review of 1965 Robert Fraser Gallery exhibition], p. 244 *in* No more an island, London. *Studio International*, Dec. 1965 (vol. 170, no. 872), pp. 242–5.

Gene Baro. [review of 1965 Robert Fraser Gallery one-man exhibition], p. 49 *in* London: a busy, vigorous season. *Arts Magazine*, Jan. 1966 (vol. 40, no. 3), pp. 45–9.

Alastair Gordon. [review of 1965 Robert Fraser Gallery one-man exhibition], p. 39 *in* Art in the modern manner. *Connoisseur*, Jan. 1966 (vol. 161, no. 647), pp. 38–9.

Robert Hughes. Blake and Hockney: [review of 1965 Robert Fraser Gallery one-man exhibition]. *London Magazine*, Jan. 1966 (vol. 5, no. 10), pp. 68–73.

Robert Melville. [review of 1965 Robert Fraser Gallery one-man exhibition], p. 147 *in* The new classicism. *Architectural Review*, Feb. 1966 (vol. 139, no. 826), pp. 145–7.

Barry Joyce. Peter Blake: Pop artist [chiefly interview]. *Modus Vivendi*: [college magazine of South-West Essex Technical College and School of Art], 31 Oct. 1966 (vol. 1, no. 1), pp. 12–14.

Artist will convert abandoned station. *Bristol Evening Post*, 26 May 1967, p. 40.

Paul Overy. [review of July 1967 Robert Fraser Gallery group exhibition] *in* On the streets (Round the art galleries). *Listener*, 13 July 1967 (vol. 78, no. 1998), p. 45.

Robert Melville. The case for Fraser: [review of July 1967 Robert Fraser Gallery group exhibition]. *New Statesman*, 14 July 1967. p. 61.

Tribute to Robert Fraser [on the occasion of the July 1967 Robert Fraser Gallery group exhibition]. *Art and Artists*, Aug. 1967 (vol. 2, no. 5), pp. 12–13.

Keith Roberts. Blake, Dine, Hamilton/Arts Council Gallery: [review of 1967/8 Arts Council Gallery, Cambridge, group exhibition]. *Varsity*, 20 Jan. 1968, p. 17.

R.C. Kenedy. [on O.U.P. display of Old Testament drawings held at Oxford University Press, Ely House, London], p. 46 *in* London letter. *Art International*, Mar. 1969 (vol. 13, no. 3), pp. 46–51.

Simon Field. [review of 1969 Robert Fraser Gallery one-man exhibition], p. 57 *in* The pleasure principle. *Art and Artists*, May 1969 (vol. 4, no. 2), pp. 56–7.

Alastair Gordon. [review of 1969 Robert Fraser Gallery one-man exhibition], p. 101 *in* Art in the modern manner. *Connoisseur*, Oct. 1969 (vol. 172, no. 692), pp. 100–101.

*Michael McNay. Blake's Jerusalem. *Guardian*, 20 Nov. 1969.

K.R. [Keith Roberts]. [review of 1969 Bristol City Art Gallery one-man exhibition]. *Burlington Magazine*, Dec. 1969 (vol. 111, no. 801), p. 781.

Robert Melville. Peter Blake and the fairies: [including review of 1969 Bristol City Art Gallery one-man exhibition]. *New Statesman*, 5 Dec. 1969 (vol. 78, no. 2021), p. 835.

F. Swann. Peter Blake: [review of 1969 Bristol City Art Gallery one-man exhibition]. *Arts Review*, 6 Dec. 1969 (vol. 21, no. 24), p. 798.

Christopher Neve. Crazy said Snow-White, Peter Blake and the pop art revolution. *Country Life*, 18 Dec. 1969, pp. 1658–60.

Roger Coleman. Peter Blake's nostalgia: [review of 1969 Bristol City Art Gallery one-man exhibition]. *Art and Artists*, Jan. 1970 (vol. 4, no. 10), pp. 30–2.

Bernard Denvir. [review of 1969 Bristol City Art Gallery one-man exhibition], pp. 79–80 *in* London letter. *Art International*, Jan. 1970 (vol. 14, no. 1), pp. 77–80.

Robert Melville. [review of 1969 Bristol City Art Gallery one-man exhibition] *in* Two romantic realists. *Architectural Review*, Feb. 1970 (vol. 147, no. 876), pp. 150–2.

Marina Vaizey. The Royal Academy exhibition [1970 Summer exhibition]. *Arts Review*, 9 May 1970 (vol. 22, no. 9), pp. 282–3.

Francis Greenacre. [acquisition by Bristol City Art Gallery of Peter Blake's drawing 'Executive Type'], p. 778 *in* Acquisitions of modern art by museums. *Burlington Magazine*, Nov. 1970 (vol. 112, no. 812), pp. 775–786.

Bernard Denvir. [review of Dec. 1970 Waddington exhibition with Graham Ovenden], p. 43 *in* London letter. *Art International*, Feb. 1971 (vol. 15, no. 2), pp. 42–45.

John Russell. [review of 1972 Waddington one-man exhibition] *in* Best of boys. *Sunday Times*, 10 Dec. 1972, p. 37.

Barbara Wright. Peter Blake: [review of 1972 Waddington one-man exhibition]. *Arts Review*, 16 Dec. 1972 (vol. 24, no. 25/26), pp. 780–1.

Nigel Gosling. [review of 1972 Waddington one-man exhibition] *in* Notions from the nursery. *Observer*, 17 Dec. 1972, p. 31.

Richard Cork. Blake's passion for the past . . . [review of 1972 Waddington one-man exhibition]. *Evening Standard*, 21 Dec. 1972, p. 25.

Antje von Graevenitz. [review of 1973 Stedlijk Museum, Amsterdam, one-man exhibition] *in* Museen und Galerien:

Niederlande. *Pantheon*, Jan./Feb./Mar. 1973 (Jahrgang 32, no. 1), p. 98.

William Feaver. [review of 1972 Waddington one-man exhibition], p. 58 *in* London letter. *Art International*, Mar. 1973 (vol. 17, no. 3), pp. 56–59.

Julian Gállego. Pintores ingleses de hoy. *in* Crónica de Paris. *Goya : revista de arte*, May–June 1973 (no. 114), pp. 364–5.

Walter Barten. Absurde machines en charmante vertelkunst : [includes review of 1973 Stedelijk Museum, Amsterdam, one-man exhibition]. *De Groene Amsterdammer*, 24 Oct. 1973.

Fanny Kelk. Popart in het Stedelijk : [review of 1973 Stedelijk Museum, Amsterdam, one-man exhibition]. *Het Parool* (Amsterdam), 26 Oct. 1973.

Peter Blake : [review of 1973 Stedelijk Museum, Amsterdam, one-man exhibition]. *De Telegraaf* (Amsterdam), 2 Nov. 1973.

Peter Fuller. Peter Blake. p. 834 *in* [Peter Fuller's Bristol/Bath supplement]. *Arts Review*, 1 Dec. 1973 (vol. 25, no. 25).

Sigrid Metken. Facteur Chevals Posttasche : die Bildpostkarte in der Kunst. *Das Kunstwerk*, Jan. 1974 (vol. 27, no. 1), pp. 3–42 (p. 7 on Peter Blake).

Peter Winter. Peter Blake : [review of 1973/4 Hamburg one-man exhibition]. *Das Kunstwerk*, Mar. 1974 (vol. 27, no. 2), pp. 44–5.

René Dalemans. Peter Blake : [review of 1974 Brussels one-man exhibition]. *in* Crónica de Bruselas. *Goya : revista de arte*, Mar.–Apr. 1974 (no. 119), pp. 309–10.

Pat Gilmour. Peter Blake print retrospective : [review of 1974 Natalie Stern one-man exhibition]. *Arts Review*, 3 May 1974 (vol. 26, no. 9), pp. 246–8.

Michael Greenwood. [review of 1974 Hayward Gallery group exhibition], p. 31 *in* British painting '74. *Artscanada*, Mar. 1975 (nos. 196/7), pp. 29–34.

Fenella Crichton. [review of Feb. 1975 Kinsman Morrison Gallery group exhibition], p. 41 *in* London letter. *Art International*, Apr. 1975 (vol. 19, no. 4), pp. 37–41.

Maurice Tuchman. European painting in the Seventies. *Art and Artists*, Nov. 1975 (vol. 10, no. 8), pp. 44–9 (p. 46 on Peter Blake).

Gerald Nordland [review of 1975 County Museum of Art, Los Angeles, group exhibition], p. 32 *in* Los Angeles newsletter. *Art International*, Dec. 1975 (vol. 19, no. 10), pp. 29–37.

Guido Ballo and Franco Russoli. Arte inglese oggi 1960–1976 : [on the occasion of the 1976 Milan group exhibition]. *Le Arti*, Apr. 1976 (vol. 26, no. 4), pp. 11–16.

Luigi Moreno and Marilù Re Fiorentin. I primi sono stati gli inglesi : chi l'ha detto che la Pop art è Americana ? : [on the occasion of the 1976 Hamburg group exhibition]. *Bolaffiarte*, Apr.–May 1976 (no. 59), pp. 32–5.

Paul Overy. Superstars for a day : the rise of Pop art in England : [review of 1976 York group exhibition]. *The Times*, 2 June 1976. p. 12.

Robert Melville. [review of Peter Blake's work in 1976 Royal Academy Summer exhibition], p. 53 *in* The word as decoration. *Architectural Review*, July 1976 (vol. 160, no. 953), pp. 51–4.

Edward Lucie-Smith. [review of Peter Blake's work in 1976 Royal Academy Summer exhibition], pp. 5–6 *in* Two academies. *Art and Artists*, July 1976 (vol. 11, no. 4), pp. 4–9.

Toni del Renzio. [review of 1976 Rotterdam group exhibition] *in* Style, technique and iconography. *Art and Artists*, July 1976 (vol. 11, no. 4), pp. 34–9.

Edward Lucie-Smith. Realism rules ! O.K. ? *Art and Artists*, Sept. 1976 (vol. 11, no. 6), pp. 8–15 (pp. 8–9 on Peter Blake).

Brian Moynahan. Brotherhood of Ruralists. *Sunday Times Magazine*, 3 Oct. 1976, pp. 78–84.

Marina Vaizey. Jim Dine and Peter Blake : [review of 1977 Waddington and Tooth Galleries one-man exhibition]. *Arts Review*, 15 Apr. 1977 (vol. 29, no. 8), pp. 253–4.

Michael Shepherd. Authority and obscurity : figuring it out : [review of 1977 Waddington and Tooth Galleries exhibition]. *Sunday Telegraph*, 1 May 1977.

William Packer. Kitaj, Dine and Blake : [review of 1977 Waddington and Tooth Galleries one-man exhibition]. *Financial Times*, 7 May 1977, p. 9.

John McEwen. [review of 1977 Waddington and Tooth Galleries one-man exhibition], p. 32 *in* Mushy. *Spectator*, 7 May 1977, pp. 31–2.

William Feaver. The Stella Collection : [review of 1977 Waddington and Tooth Galleries exhibition]. *Observer*, 8 May 1977, p. 28.

Marina Vaizey. A world of self-portraits : [review of 1977 Waddington and Tooth exhibition]. *Sunday Times*, 8 May 1977. p. 38.

Fenella Crichton. [review of 1977 Waddington and Tooth exhibition], p. 73 *in* London letter. *Art International*, May–June 1977 (vol. 21, no. 3), pp. 69–73.

Keith Roberts. [review of 1977 Waddington and Tooth exhibition], p. 460 *in* Current and forthcoming exhibitions : London. *Burlington Magazine*, June 1977 (vol. 119, no. 891), pp. 459–63.

The Brotherhood of Ruralists (Town and country). *Country Life*, 23 June 1977, p. 173.

Edward Lucie-Smith. [review of 1977 Waddington and Tooth exhibition], p. 10 *in* In view. *Art and Artists*, July 1977 (vol. 12, no. 4), pp. 4–10.

John Sansom. Art in focus : [on the Ruralists]. *Bristol and West Country Illustrated*, July 1977, pp. 16–7.

Richard Cork. Tisdall, Cork and Overy are framed in Hayward Annual Part Two. Peter Blake's open letter, hanging at the Arts Council Summer Show, shows the successful school of British artists on the defensive : [Peter Blake's open letter and Richard Cork's response]. *Guardian*, 20 July 1977, p. 10. Elicited replies in the Guardian from Janet Daley (21 July); Phillip Gill (22 July); Francis Golding, Norbert Lynton and Paul Overy (23 July); Jean Bawden (25 July); John Hoyland (26 July); David Hockney, Patrick Heron and Alan Lowndes

(28 July); and Guardian Editorial (3rd leader) 1 Aug. 1977 (q.v.).

Art critics and first principles: [Editorial, 3rd leader, on Peter Blake's correspondence on art critics]. *Guardian*, 1 Aug. 1977, p. 10.

William Feaver. [review of Brotherhood of Ruralists exhibition, 1977]. *Observer*, 4 Sept. 1977, p. 7.

Edward Lucie-Smith. [review of Brotherhood of Ruralists exhibition, 1977], pp. 41–2 *in* Scotland the brave. *Art and Artists*, Oct. 1977 (vol. 12, no. 6), pp. 40–3.

Andy Christian. Painters bud in city schools, blossom in the country: England's 'Brotherhood of Ruralists'. *Christian Science Monitor*, 8 Jan. 1979, p. 21.

Rosalind Thuillier. Peter Blake [review of 1979 Bohun Gallery one-man exhibition]. *Arts Review*, 13 Apr. 1979 (vol. 31, no. 7), p. 192.

Prints and photographs published. Peter Blake, 'Side-show' (1974–9): a series of five wood engravings . . . *Print Collector's Newsletter*, July–Aug. 1979 (vol. 10, no. 3), p. 92.

*R. Pincus. Contemporizing the figure: Peter Blake, R.B. Kitaj, L.A.[sic] Auerbach, Francis Bacon, Leon Kossoff: [review of 1979 Louver Gallery exhibition]. *Artweek*, 15 Dec. 1979 (vol. 10, no. 42), p. 16.

M. Rothenstein. Acceleration from zero. *Print Review*, no. 12, 1980, pp. 24–35.

Ian Dury [interviewed on Peter Blake]. *New Musical Express*, 19 July 1980, pp. 27–28.

Rod Chaytor. Art row over a packet of fags: £1,800 up in smoke. *Daily Mirror*, 15 Aug. 1980, p. 7.

James O'Brien. Council may spend £1,800 on painting of cigarette packet. *Daily Telegraph*, 15 Aug. 1980, p. 2.

Council's proposed pop art purchase angers Tories. *The Times*, 15 Aug. 1980, p. 2.

Lewis Biggs. The Ruralists. *Arnolfini Review* (Bristol), Apr. 1981, pp. 1–2.

Marina Vaizey. Elegy for a country garden: [review of 1981 Brotherhood of Ruralists exhibition]. *Sunday Times*, 19 Apr. 1981, p. 41.

William Packer. Ruralists [review of 1981 Brotherhood of Ruralists exhibition]. *Financial Times*, 21 Apr. 1981, p. 19.

Caroline Odgers. A move to the country: the Brotherhood of Ruralists. *Country Life*, 23 Apr. 1981, pp. 1112–3.

Kate Flint. Cricket and crab-apples: [review of 1981 Brotherhood of Ruralists exhibition]. *Times Literary Supplement*, 1 May 1981 (no. 4074), p. 466.

Terry Grimley. The Ruralists: [review of the 1981 Brotherhood of Ruralists exhibition]. *Birmingham Post*, 3 June 1981.

Clare Henry. Painters akin to nature: [review of 1981 Brotherhood of Ruralists exhibition]. *Glasgow Herald*, 24 July 1981.

Emilio Coia. Rural touch at the Third Eye: [review of 1981 Brotherhood of Ruralists exhibition]. *Scotsman*, 27 July 1981.

John Michell. The Ruralists: [review of the 1981 Brotherhood of Ruralists exhibition]. *Resurgence*, July–Aug. 1981 (no. 87), pp. 8–9.

Linda Talbot. Something devilish in Devizes: [review of the 1981 Brotherhood of Ruralists exhibition]. *Hampstead & Highgate Express*, 21 August 1981 (no. 6294), p. 54.

Jules Lubbock. What grounds?: [review of 1981 Brotherhood of Ruralists exhibition]. *New Statesman*, 4 Sept. 1981, p. 24.

William Feaver. Tinkerbell lives . . . on the Brotherhood of Ruralists [exhibition at the Camden Art Centre, 1981]. *Observer*, 6 Sept. 1981, p. 25.

Peter Blake in retrospect: [interview with Mike von Joel]. *Art Line*, no. 2, Nov. 1982, pp. 5–7.

Emma Parsons. Peter Blake interviewed. *Arts Review Year Book*, 1983, pp. 46–7.